Teaching Powerful Writing

25 Short Read-Aloud Stories With Lessons That Motivate Students to Use Literary Elements in Their Writing

by Bob Sizoo

SCHOLASTIC
PROFESSIONAL BOOKS

NEW YORK • TORONTO • LONDON • AUCKLAND • SYDNEY
MEXICO CITY • NEW DELHI • HONG KONG • BUENOS AIRES

Dedication

To Sue, whose ear for language and mastery of conventions make her my editor
of first resort, and who reminds me that sometimes the best way to improve
my teaching is to take a walk in the forest.

Cover design by Norma Ortiz
Interior design by LDL Designs
Cover and interior photographs by Tina Mori

ISBN 0-439-11111-0

Acknowledgments

I imagine answering a multiple-choice test 16 years ago containing only the following question:

What are you least *likely to be doing in sixteen years:*
  a) Playing centerfield for the Dodgers
  b) Singing the part of Aida at the Met
  c) Living luxuriously on your lottery winnings
  d) Writing a book

Even if I weren't 50 and lacking in all but the most rudimentary baseball talent, as a Giants fan, I wouldn't play for the Dodgers; my natural four-note range falls between bass and baritone; and I know I'm more likely to be hit by lightning than I am to win the lottery. Nevertheless, I would have chosen "d." I hated writing in school. Even in college, if I had a choice between writing a paper and taking a final, the test was always the least painful of the two. What happened?

In 1986, I had a lunchtime discussion with Lynn Strope, one of my fellow teachers at Lincoln School in Eureka, California. We shared some of our writing lessons and practices but agreed that we would like to strengthen our teaching in that area. "I've heard the writing project is good," she said. We both applied for and were accepted to the Redwood Writing Project Summer Institute for 1987 (see next page). My teaching and writing haven't been the same since.

In 1988, I began codirecting the Redwood Writing Project with Susan Bennett, an English professor at Humboldt State University. Susan has encouraged me to become a better writer in order to improve the writing of my students. Her coaching and response to my writing have been invaluable to me and to every teacher who has attended our summer institute over the last 13 years. That 13 of the 25 read-alouds in this book are written by teachers associated with the Redwood Writing Project attests to her influence.

I began my relationship with Donald Graves long before we met. His book, *Writing: Teachers and Children at Work*, has been required reading since the early '80s for any teacher who wanted to engage students in writing. Since meeting Don and working on a piece for *Instructor* magazine with him several years ago, I count on his opinions and feedback to stimulate my thinking about writing, teaching, politics, relationships, and baseball. Don shares responsibility for inspiring this book. At the International Reading Association (IRA) conference in Orlando in 1998, he and I drove to a Mexican restaurant on the outskirts of town for a quiet lunch and some catching up. He brought along his hot-off-the-press book, *How to Catch a Shark*, and read a couple of selections aloud to me during lunch. One of them was about his Uncle Nelson. He then told me another story about Uncle Nelson. I loved the story and thought it was a great example of a firsthand biographical sketch. It's the one called "The Cut Anchor Line" in this book.

At the same IRA conference a couple of days later, I had dinner with my friend Wendy Murray. Wendy had been an editor at *Instructor* when I worked on the Donald Graves article but was then, as she is now, an editor with Scholastic Professional Books. At one point in our conversation she said, "Pitch me a book." I was initially taken aback.

"I don't think we need another book about how to teach writing," I replied. "If teachers can't read Don Graves, Nancie Atwell, Lucy Calkins, Donald Murray, Regie Routman, Ralph Fletcher, and

Shelley Harwayne and figure out how to do a good job teaching writing, there's nothing much I can tell them. Besides, I'm working on writing stories, right now."

"What kind of stories?" she asked.

"Autobiographical incidents. Ones I can read aloud to my class as examples. I have a few, but I need more. You don't want a book of stories, do you?"

"That depends, tell me about them."

So I began telling Wendy about my stories and how I was collecting them along with pieces written by other teachers. And how Don Graves had told me a story a couple of days earlier that would fit perfectly. And before I knew it, I was beginning to describe what is now this book. Wendy told me she thought it was a good idea, and I should write it up in a proposal. The rest, as they say, is history.

Wendy not only helped provide me with the momentum to write this book, but her input improved the result greatly. She has demonstrated to me that good editing and good teaching of writing are alike; by providing suggestions and responses instead of corrections, she has allowed me to remain the author. My authority would be far less without her.

I'd like to thank the current and resting members of my writing group, John, Bick, Mindy, Mary, Will, Linda, Cherie, and Martha. I hope you like our book!

Finally, I would like to thank all the students who have spent their precious time with me in room seventeen at Lincoln School. They have shown me that if I just hone my observation and listening skills, they'll teach me almost everything I need to know to become a good teacher. I'm working on it.

The National Writing Project Summer Institute

At the first session of the summer institute, I noticed something different about this "class" from every other class I'd taken on the Humboldt State University campus—it was co-taught by Karen Carlton, a university English professor, and Judy Dixon, a middle school teacher. This design was intentional; throughout the summer institute we frequently examined connections between current research and theory and the classroom practices of both the codirectors and the teacher-participants. We were told that the model of this institute was one of teachers teaching teachers, and not one of the more top-down design we were used to from our education classes in the university.

National Writing Project Summer Institutes invite teachers from kindergarten through college to participate. This seemed strange at first. Teacher inservice is usually split up by grade levels or at least has lots of time for grade-level discussion. But learning to write is a recursive process. All writers can gather ideas, compose, revise, edit, and publish. Sue Grafton may sell books all over the world while Susie Kindergartener may publish an exclusive edition on the refrigerator door, but they may well have gone through corresponding steps to get to a finished piece. The steps are the same; they just get a little more sophisticated with each iteration. Thus, I learned teaching strategies useful to my sixth-grade teaching from the kindergarten teachers at the institute as well as from the college composition instructor who attended that summer.

Not only did we share our teaching successes and challenges in order to improve our teaching, but we worked on our own writing. As the directors explained to their somewhat reluctant audience, you wouldn't take your child to a piano teacher who couldn't play the piano. After overcoming my initial revulsion at writing with peers, I discovered something: after writing to prompts, meeting in a writing response group with other teachers, sharing my work and listening to other teachers share theirs with the whole group, and learning to pay close attention to voice, audience, and purpose, my writing improved. As importantly to my teaching, I began to get hung up at some of the same places in my writing that snagged my students. I returned to my teaching that fall with not only a renewed vigor for teaching writing but with more empathy for some of the problems my students were having and more experience at coping with those problems.

The National Writing Project holds summer institutes at 167 sites around the United States, in Puerto Rico, and even in a few other countries, all following the model established by the original Bay Area Writing Project in 1973: teachers teaching teachers. I recommend you join me and many of the authors in this collection in an NWP institute next summer. Contact information is listed in the "Resources" section on page 117.

TABLE OF CONTENTS

◇◇◇◇◇◇◇◇◇◇◇◇◇◇◇

INTRODUCTION

A few years ago I heard Jim Trelease, author of the excellent *Read Aloud Handbook,* speak to a group of teachers about the benefits of reading aloud literature with students. Trelease recalled a time when a high school teacher once asked him why he should read aloud when his students already know how to read for themselves. Trelease's daughter had studied for a year at Oxford and every session of her English literature class began with the professor reading aloud. After pointing this out, Trelease asked the high school teacher what he knew about the uselessness of reading aloud that the Oxford professor did not. Based on my experiences as a sixth-grade teacher, and as a guest in numerous other classrooms, I'll side with Trelease on this issue.

When you read aloud to your students, they encounter people and places they otherwise wouldn't and discover as yet unrealized opportunities to connect with the world. We often witness the damage done by teens who haven't found their places in the world—damage done both to themselves and to our communities. Through stories, they see that they aren't the only ones who struggle with finding an identity, experience conflict with peers and family, make decisions that are foolish or naive, and encounter pain, embarrassment, success, and defeat.

Reading aloud is a welcome ritual for middle school students. As Nancie Atwell says in her book *In the Middle:* "For a long time I thought of reading aloud as something teachers in the elementary grades did to entertain young children. But from my [middle school] students' responses to texts I read aloud in minilessons, I learned this wasn't at all true."

Reading aloud affects students in more concrete ways as well. John Shefflebine, a longtime systematic phonics advocate, promotes reading aloud to students of all ages as the best way to build academic vocabulary. By hearing language used at a level of sophistication beyond their independent reading levels, students learn the language of books and extend their own facility with words. Hearing the phrasing and pacing of experienced readers helps students to make sense of the text. Stories read aloud can both acquaint students with previously unknown words and bring meaning into words they vaguely understand.

Reading aloud gives an entire classroom a common text to use in a discussion or mini-lesson about elements of literature. How does Mildred Taylor's use of dialect help establish setting in *Roll of Thunder, Hear My Cry?* What does Will's dilemma in *The White Mountains* say about the theme of individual freedom? How does Maniac McGee's character change after he moves to the other side of the tracks? All teachers who read aloud have asked these kinds of questions while reading to their classes.

Not only do students improve reading skills when they hear more advanced text read aloud, but they become better writers as well. They learn more about an author's word and stylistic choices. They learn to think more about voice, audience, and the purpose of writing. Teachers can help illuminate these potential lessons by pointing out exemplary features of texts as they read aloud to their students and by asking them to look at their own writing while considering those features.

One can focus on these qualities while reading longer pieces, but teachable moments can interrupt the flow of a novel only so often before the plot's current slows to a trickle. Furthermore, while novels can be illuminating, suspenseful, and entertaining, they all have one thing in common: they're all long. Not too many teachers will finish reading aloud *The Cay,* and say, "Now you've heard an example of a novel. Your turn. You write one." Novels are not a genre that most K–12 students will attempt. This disconnect between what students hear/read and what they're asked to write often leads them to think: That's easy for her, she's a writer, or Writers write books; I write assignments.

I'd often wished I had some examples to share with my students that were of a length they could have seen as attainable in their own writing, and in a genre they could try, but had been unable to find an anthology of such pieces. I had a few pieces I had written and samples I collected from colleagues who had attended the Redwood Writing Project summer institute. I knew that similar efforts were being made each summer at the 160 other National Writing Project sites, and invited teacher participants from all across the country to submit their writing for this book. I'm pleased with the resulting collection; I hope you will be, too.

I have chosen pieces using criteria that I feel will best encourage writing.

◇ Each piece takes 5 to 10 minutes to read aloud. Any longer, we would be tempted to interrupt the flow of the story and make our infamous teaching points. If the piece is too short, there's no time for the story to develop.

◇ Every selection is in the form of either an autobiographical incident or a firsthand biographical sketch. These forms tend to exemplify the ways in which real learning takes place in everyday life. They show that the lessons we learn are not always taught by those people in front of the class holding the chalk, and they show that the primary responsibility to master any lesson lies with the learner. These genres are approachable by all students. Autobiographical incidents require experience plus reflection. A firsthand biographical sketch requires an interaction with someone who has affected one's attitudes, behavior, or beliefs. All students are experts in living their lives. These genres are also often chosen for standardized writing assessments. Need I say more?

◇ Nearly every composition is written by a teacher. I think it's important for students to see that we teachers have had experiences in life other than standing in a classroom in sensible shoes with a gaggle of people decades younger than ourselves. You may have experienced meeting a student at the local grocery or department store, and seeing the student look at you wide-eyed, realizing that you actually go out and mingle with the community. I sometimes wonder if students think we go home to Mars when we're not at school.

◇ Most importantly, every story in this collection is a well-told, engaging piece of writing. In both of these genres, as in good fiction, character is king. If the reader doesn't care what happens to the character, the plot is irrelevant. In an autobiographical incident the writer shows how important parts of his or her life converge in a single moment. In a firsthand biographical sketch, the author shows how important moments were affected by a single person. In both, the key is to show the importance.

To make the collection more useful to the classroom teacher, each composition includes a brief note from the author explaining some background or problems encountered while writing the piece. Each piece also includes teaching ideas that focus on a specific strength of the piece, encouraging students to experiment in their own writing. These aren't scripted lessons, however. In many I suggest that students "think about" or "discuss" an idea or topic. It's up to the teacher to translate the suggestion into an appropriate structure (mini-lesson, pair share, small-group or whole-class discussion, reflect in a journal, write a letter, set up a classroom debate, and so on).

I have attempted to put together a tool that is useful to teachers of all styles and methodologies. If you do full-blown writer's and/or reader's workshops, I hope the mini-lesson suggestions fit your classroom well. If you teach with a more traditional style, I encourage you to discover effective assignments within. At the very least, I invite you to enjoy reading these stories written by your fellow teachers.

In the next three chapters, I describe the context in which I use the selections that follow. Learning to Write in Room 17 explains the strategies students use all year long to write in all genres. Writing Our Lives describes teaching approaches I use to encourage students to write in a specific genre using personal narrative as an example. The assessment chapter contains strategies I use to encourage students to participate in the evaluation process, the single best strategy to improve student learning in any *subject* area.

To imagine an audience for this book, I've pictured myself in a National Writing Project summer institute discussing my teaching successes and challenges with twenty other teachers, saying, "Here are some strategies that seem to be working. You might want to try some; maybe they'll work for you, too."

CHAPTER 1:
LEARNING TO WRITE IN ROOM 17

Each September, I give the "Here are my expectations" speech to my students about their commitment to writing. It begins something like this: "I wrote quite a bit in the sixth grade. As a teacher I have read thousands of examples of sixth-grade writing. Through these experiences I have a pretty good idea of what strong sixth-grade writing looks like and what weak sixth-grade writing looks like. I also know how to make weak writing stronger. I don't need to learn this. You do." At this point some students begin to squirm. I continue, "I cannot follow you around in seventh grade and beyond to tell you if your writing is any good and how to improve it. Beginning now, you need to make a strong commitment to learning this for yourself."

During the school year my students learn to improve their writing by using many strategies, any of which could be the focus of an entire chapter or, in most cases, its own book. I'll touch on each briefly.

After reading aloud a personal narrative, Bob and his students discuss the author's intent, use of language, and other literary elements.

STUDENTS WATCH ME STRUGGLE TO COMPOSE AND REVISE

Often a writing mini-lesson consists of students watching me write on an overhead, while I speak aloud my thoughts. I may be choosing a topic by creating a list, clustering, or simply writing down the things I did over the weekend. I'll then scan what I've written and discuss various writing possibilities. For example, maybe I took a walk in the woods and almost got run down by a college student on a mountain bike. I could write an opinion piece on rules and regulations in the community forest, an analytical essay discussing the possible physical and psychological needs people satisfy by spending a day in the forest, a piece of nature writing about the forest ecosystem, or a poem about the promise of spring inspired by the first trilium blossom of the year. Donald Graves calls this reflective process "reading the world." For an in-depth description of this technique, see Graves's *Fresh Voices*.

Sometimes I'll show students the struggle in the revision process by projecting that week's parent letter on the overhead. We then examine sentence length, structure of the letter, word choice, and content to see what could be changed, left out, or added. I may read aloud a story I'm working on and ask the class to help me with areas in which I'm struggling: "Do you think the foreshadowing gives away too much?" or "I've told this story in a linear fashion. Do you think it would be stronger if I moved the park scene to the beginning and tell the earlier events in the story as a flashback?"

We'll also edit my writing on the overhead for spelling, punctuation, grammar, and capitalization. I've tried writing intentionally flawed pieces for this purpose, but it doesn't work. The students always see that I dumbed down the writing for them, which offends them and completely ruins the spirit of shared inquiry. Instead of genuinely asking them for advice, they see that I'm trying to ask them about something I already know. My writing is flawed enough so that an unedited draft leaves plenty of room for improvement. Students feel a greater sense of accomplishment by actually helping me improve my writing than they do by participating in an exercise.

Bob in the midst of a mini-lesson demonstrating that *a lot* is two words.

Another effective way to examine conventions is to put student work on the overhead. Early in the year I use the anonymous work of students from previous years. As the year progresses, students gain courage and volunteer to let us edit their work as a class. They know their pieces improve through response from the entire class and enjoy the fellowship they experience when their classmates take time to look carefully at their work.

STUDENTS SHARE THEIR WORK

My students share their work in the author's chair, in fishbowls, during informal discussions, in peer response groups, in conference with me or a classroom volunteer, and reading aloud to their second-grade study buddies.

Author's chair is reserved for finished work. I keep a sign-up sheet for the author's chair posted in our writing center (see Appendix). Depending on the number of students who sign up and the state of my classroom schedule, I'll either feature authors one at a time (usually after recess or lunch), or schedule 15 to 20 minutes of author's chair, allowing four or five students time to share.

Students often share their work with the class informally. After students write to a prompt (see page 14), I'll ask, "Who wants to share what you've come up with?" At the end of a writers' workshop, I ask students to search through their current piece and find a "golden line" to read aloud to the class. I may ask them to find a sentence or paragraph that they changed from a previous draft, or one that sounds clunky to them, which they want to change in the next draft. Giving students time to read a portion of their works in progress allows those who may be reluctant to sit in the author's chair an opportunity to participate successfully.

Fishbowls are simply three students—an author and two classmates—modeling a peer response group in front of the class. The author reads aloud the piece once while the respondents just listen. (Because students are revising for content, not conventions at this stage, only the author needs a copy of the piece.) Then the respondents write their initial impression of the piece. The author reads aloud the piece a second time, but this time the respondents take notes while listening. In a fishbowl, not only are the two students in the front of the class taking notes but so is everyone else in the room.

The first few times we do fishbowls, I ask all students to write on a peer response form (see page 121). In the "+" column they record things they like about the piece. In the "-/?" column they comment on weaknesses or places in the writing where they get confused or have questions. Every student has to write at least three responses in each column. After the writer reads the piece for the second time, the respondents read aloud their notes. The writer may not defend or clarify the piece, only take notes. Thus, when one student says, "I got confused during the part that took place in the kitchen, and the character began brushing his teeth," the author doesn't explain the scene, but makes notes to remember to clarify the scene in the next draft.

After the writer reads and both respondents in the fishbowl have given their responses, something magical happens. I ask, "How many of you heard a comment from one of the group members that was similar to one you wrote on your paper?" Invariably, every hand is raised. Then I ask, "Who wrote a comment that has not been mentioned yet?" Several students in the audience then get a chance to give their two cents. Not only does the author get reinforcement that the comments may be valid, but the class is beginning to understand that the qualities of good writing are not such a mystery after all. They're actually beginning to recognize those qualities.

In fishbowls we learn the language of response. We learn that we're commenting on the text, not on the writer. We learn that "It's good," or "That stinks," doesn't help the writer improve the piece. Specificity rules. What is good about it? Where in the story do you get confused? What are you noticing about the author's use of language? Where and how does the author paint a clear picture of the setting? Which characters are well drawn, and which need to be more fully developed? Where do you need more details to clarify the story? Our extensive practice in fishbowls helps students begin to look critically at their own work.

We may do fishbowls for two weeks to three months, depending on the class, before I divide them into groups of three to work in peer response groups independently for the first time. I assign the groups heterogeneously, with no "best friends" together. Only one person speaks at a time in the peer response group method we use, so if any group is engaged in social conversation, I know they're off task and call them back into a whole group setting. Then I'll say something teacherly like, "With the freedom to work with your peers comes the responsibility to be productive. It appears that you need closer supervision and would rather have me yammer at you." This is a strategic point at which to take out the grammar textbooks.

Though I begin peer response groups wielding an iron glove, eventually students realize that being on task in a peer response group is more productive and rewarding than being on task with an

Students discuss the elements of a genre; in this case, fairy tales.

ancient grammar textbook. Once they see their own writing and the writing of their classmates improve, they actually look forward to the response to and from their peers. In the "best" years the entire class only meets in the response groups I organize a few times. After they become proficient and productive in the process, I use a sign-up sheet similar to the one for author's chair (see page 122). When three students have signed up on the sheet to get response to the piece on which they are working, they meet in a response group independently during writing time.

STUDENTS KEEP A WRITING FOLDER AND A WRITER'S NOTEBOOK

My students save all their written work for the entire school year in hanging file folders. In time, they organize their work into a folder for works in progress and another for finished pieces. This chronological record is especially useful when I ask students to find examples of their work that show growth through the school year.

In writer's notebooks, students record ideas that might otherwise slip away. They revisit these ideas, and either develop them or leave them to percolate a while. I tell them it's a diary of their writing life—a place to record thoughts when they are thinking like writers. Entries may include responses to prompts, lists of potential character names, future writing topics, lists or descriptions of settings, quotes from authors they are reading, overheard conversations, or snippets of dialogue or description that "just come to them." They may want to incorporate their notebook entries into later work; they may not. Most importantly, the ideas are there, and students who keep an active writer's notebook never say, "I don't know what to write about." Sometimes I ask students to share their notebooks with me and to show me how they're learning to think like writers. I never grade the notebooks for spelling, complete sentences, or other conventions. It's a fluency tool.

STUDENTS RESPOND TO MINI-LESSONS OR PROMPTS

Few issues engender more discussion among writing teachers than the use of prompts. "It gives my kids something to write about," say the pro-prompters. "Why stifle them? Teach them to choose their own topics," reply the anti-prompters. I use quality prompts, but employ them sparingly.

What is a "quality" prompt? I don't mean a "fun" prompt. Oftentimes, we teachers, in an effort to make school less painful for our students, glom on to an activity because we think it'll be fun for them. We have to be careful that we aren't thinking about fun primarily, and learning secondarily. As I tell my students, "School is your job." After all, when was the last time your principal said to you at a staff meeting, "I want you do something new because I think it'll be fun for you." Sometimes school's work.

To identify a quality prompt, I ask myself, "Does responding to this prompt increase students' writing independence?" "Story starters" increase dependence. When every student's story begins, "The spaceship landed. Out walked…," or "'Good morning,' said Mr. Daffodil…" students are completing someone else's story. I want them to write their own. For example, if I want to teach my students about personification, I'm not going start everyone with the aforementioned Mr. Daffodil. Justin may have noticed that very morning a beautiful yellow daffodil popping up in his yard. He may be anxious to give voice to that new resident of his home. But some students haven't seen a daffodil lately or don't even know what a daffodil is. For them, it's just more writing for an audience of one, the teacher.

Rather, my approach is to give a mini-lesson explaining to students that sometimes authors use personification to make their writing more engaging, and to give them some examples. I may read a picture book in which the author uses personification: Virginia Lee Burton's *The Little House* in which a house in the country wonders about city life, or William Steig's *Yellow and Pink* in which two marionettes discuss their plights. For the writing part of the lesson I'll prompt my students by saying, "Think of an object in your life that is meaningful to you and give it a voice. Engage that object in a conversation with you, a friend, family member or another human, or even another object." Then they're on their own for a while. Justin may indeed be writing about a talking daffodil, but he'll be experimenting with personification through his story, not mine.

This is not to say that books of writing prompts are without value. I own several such books. I could write to a different prompt every day until I die and never use up my collection of prompts. I have scanned many of them for open-ended prompts that increase student independence and even used several with my classes. The real value of these books is to put them in the writing-center library with the style manuals and dictionaries. Students often scan them for writing ideas. Used in this way, a student may find just the right prompt to start writing.

STUDENTS LISTEN TO LITERATURE READ ALOUD

When we begin the study of a particular type of writing, I start by immersing my students in that genre. I'll check out relevant books from the school library and keep them in my room for my students' perusal. I'll distribute appropriate magazine articles and read aloud examples. If we're doing a genre study of nature writing, I'll read articles from *Ranger Rick* and whole or portions of articles from *Audubon, National Geographic,* or *Outside* magazines. If we're doing poetry, we'll read and study poems of all kinds. In the past, we've studied personal narrative using pieces I've written, stories I've collected from my colleagues, examples from collections of autobiographical incidents such as *Knots on a Yo-yo String* by Jerry Spinelli, and excerpts from longer autobiographical pieces that stand alone. But collecting these pieces was work. Now, we'll use the pieces in this book. After reading aloud each of these passages, we'll discuss the authors' use of language, organizational strategies, and the focus of the writing.

STUDENTS READ INDEPENDENTLY—THE MORE, THE BETTER

We read silently for 30 to 45 minutes a day. All of us. The majority of my students' homework is independent reading. Many educators, myself among them, believe one of the best ways to increase reading comprehension and writing skill is to read self-selected material independently, and often.

STUDENTS BEGIN TO READ LIKE WRITERS

Reading widely and frequently is important, but just reading won't necessarily improve writing. Do you know anyone who is a great reader, but an uninspired or unskilled writer? I'm fascinated by the connection between reading and writing, and I believe skilled readers and writers have one great reflective process in common—thinking about author's choices. It's obvious to consider word choice while writing; the metacognitive task is to put yourself in the position of reader: How can I phrase this sentence so it comes out the way I'd most enjoy reading it? What words can I use so that my audience will best understand what I'm thinking? Even as our own audience, when we're scribbling in a diary or writing down a grocery list, we always write from a reader's point of view.

Even so, to read as a writer is not so obvious a task. One reason we love our favorite authors is the word choices they make. Unless we are modeling a think-aloud for our students, we rarely consciously think, "What a great way to say that. I wonder how else the author could have said the same thing." "I don't really like the way the author said that; how could she have said it differently?" or "How would I have said that?"

In a workshop a few years ago, Lucy Calkins quoted Mortimer Adler who disagreed with the common wisdom that a good book is one you can't put down. Adler said, "A good book is one you have to put down." A couple of years later, I was sitting in the shade of a Douglas fir on the banks of the Mattole River reading *God of Small Things* when the protagonist, Ammu, encountered futility in her life. Arundhati Roy wrote, "It seemed so

A short conference can help a student get past a writing hurdle.

absurd. So futile. Like polishing firewood." The book fell closed on my lap. What a metaphor (okay, technically a simile). What other metaphors for futility could an author use? Like leaving your front door open for 15 minutes on a hot day so your air conditioner will cool off the neighborhood before you walk to the market. Like giving a reading comprehension test to a child who doesn't speak English to judge one's teaching efficacy.

I realized I was validating Adler's claim; I had to put the book down. And I knew I was reading like a writer. I want my students to do this—to bring to the mental forefront the reflective task of reading. Without consciously (at least at first) thinking about improving one's writing by reading, it won't happen. We can't just read; we have to read like a writer.

When my students write, I ask them to consider the audience—to write like a reader. Reading aloud exemplary pieces to them, I encourage them to reverse the relationship—to read like a writer. We look for places in the piece where the author had to make a decision about form or the use of language, and we use that point as a springboard for discussion. When students see that real authors are constantly faced with real choices and don't just record words dictated by their muse, they begin to see themselves as potential writers.

CHAPTER 2: WRITING OUR LIVES

Personal narrative can take many forms. Young children often write about themselves by listing attributes or preferences. "I have brown eyes. I have red hair. I like pizza. I like my dog. I like soccer." As writers become more sophisticated, personal narrative may take the form of a composed reflection. Typical titles may be, "Julie, My Best Friend" or "Why I Like Camping." In this stage, students will gather some evidence to support their theses, but these narratives are often unreflective, emotional pieces that lack description, organizing structures, and focus.

I ask my students to share their life stories in two rather specific genres: autobiographical incident and firsthand biographical sketch. Aside from sharing attributes with all good writing, these two genres have much in common and a couple of features unique to each.

Many teachers call an autobiographical incident a "crystal moment." The writer describes a moment that stands out vividly. One of a writer's most important tasks is to show the reader why that moment is particularly important. This is difficult for students; they often want to tell the reader, "I was so scared," or "It was very embarrassing," instead of showing those things through description or dialogue.

The firsthand biographical sketch holds similar importance, but instead of an important moment, it concentrates on an influential person. As with the autobiographical incident, the writer must show us the importance of the relationship being examined, not tell us. In Donald Graves's piece in this book, he never says, "Uncle Nelson was really important to me." Instead, Graves shows the reader this importance by carefully describing Uncle Nelson's skillful work and his interactions and conversations with those around him.

We can't teach students to write in a genre by telling them the quality criteria any more than posting the Ten Commandments will assure that students will not covet their neighbor's Walkman. We have to teach by example and by demonstration. As I do with any genre, I begin the study of personal narrative by immersing students in examples, such as those which make up the bulk of this book. After reading aloud the first selection, I get out a piece of chart paper and ask my class to help me list attributes that add strength to writing in the piece they just heard. I'll then read a second selection, and ask what strengths that piece had in common with the first, and if, while listening to the second piece, they thought of any new attributes to record on the chart paper. On subsequent days, after reading aloud more examples, I'll ask, "Did you hear anything else in that story that we should add to the list?" By the time I've read aloud 10 or 12 selections, the list gets quite extensive.

The list for the type of personal narrative may look like this:
   ◇ There is very little telling by the author, mostly showing.
   ◇ Usually told in the first person.

◇ A beginning that captures the reader's interest.

◇ There are varied sentence lengths.

◇ It's complete—the reader can read through the story without getting lost.

◇ The pace is good—it slows down and speeds up in the right places.

◇ Clear description of important features of the setting or objects in the scene.

◇ Creates suspense or tension—we want to know what happens next.

◇ Uses dialogue or interior monologue to tell the story.

◇ Includes sensory details—sounds, smells, textures, sights, and/or tastes.

◇ Often uses some figurative or symbolic language (similes, metaphors, analogies, imagery).

◇ We learn about the character's thoughts and feelings at the time of the incident.

The list for autobiographical incident may also include:

◇ The event's significance to the author is made clear.

◇ Events may take place before or after the incident, but they should all add to the reader's understanding of the incident.

◇ Often the importance of the incident may not be clear until later in the author's life.

The list for firsthand biographical sketch may also include:

◇ The writer shows why the character is important to him/her.

◇ The writer learns something from the character.

◇ The character comes alive in the story by describing his/her habits, activities, dialogue, and looks (including dress, size, features, and so on).

◇ The character is compared and contrasted to others in the story.

After we've added to our Attributes of Writing Quality chart three or four times, I check the list to see if there is any crucial attribute students might have left out. For instance, if no student has suggested that each piece has an interesting beginning, I'll ask, "Is it important that the piece have an interesting beginning? Should we add that to our list?" Even though it is their list, I want to make sure they don't leave anything out.

After a couple of weeks or so, students have seen me work on the overhead with my own attempts in a genre, heard stories read aloud, and written in response to craft lessons based on those stories. They have completed a rough draft in the genre, written on every other line on notebook paper. I point to the chart they've created and say, "There's your revision guide. Examine your rough draft in relation to the Attribute Chart. Decide what to do to make the piece better. Make notes to yourself on your draft." Though I sometimes encourage them to do this step in pairs, it is the next revision, not this rough draft, that they take to a formal peer response group (as described on pages 12–14).

The Attribute Chart next comes into play in the assessment portion of this genre study, as described in Chapter 3. The chart remains up on the wall for easy reference.

CHAPTER 3:
ASSESSING OUR WRITING

Every July during the final week of the Redwood Writing Project Summer Institute, 20 teachers devote a morning to discussing assessment, evaluation, and grading. It's always the most animated and passionate morning of the institute, and invariably gives rise to more questions than answers.

"Does an 'A' in my class mean the same as an 'A' in your class?"

"Do I evaluate my students' writing in relationship to the rest of the students in my class, in my city, or in the entire nation?"

"How do my students' scores on norm-referenced tests affect my teaching of writing?"

"What about effort? I have highly skilled students who goof off and produce mediocre writing far below their abilities. I also have low-skilled students who devote a ton of effort and produce similar work. Do they deserve the same grade?"

The answers to many such questions about assessment, evaluation, and grading are often idiosyncratic to states, districts, schools, and even teachers. Throw in standardized testing and the conversation often becomes more political than pedagogical. I'll try to keep this chapter focused on one question: How do we use assessment to help students become better writers? I believe we do this by employing authentic assessment methods. By authentic assessment, I mean two things: Involve students in assessment, and use assessment tools and processes that inform your teaching.

KIDS EVALUATE THEIR OWN WRITING

Near the end of each grading period, I ask students to pick three pieces from their writing folders that demonstrate their very best work. They then look at the Writing Assessment Scale (see pages 123 and 124) stapled into the front of their folders and, looking for the criteria on the scale, evaluate their writing. They report their findings on the Student Self-Assessment form (see page 125).

The Writing Assessment Scale is a translation of the rubric on our district's report cards into more kid-friendly language. It's not designed to look at individual assignments, nor to judge writing ability through a grade-level lens. Rather, this scale attempts to look at the big picture of writing ability—from the nonwriter through the professional writer. At conference time I tell parents that if their kids can write at level 4 (competent writer), they should do fine in seventh-grade language arts. If they get to level 6, they can make a living using their writing skills. This reinforces the idea that there is always something to learn in becoming a good writer—there's always room for improvement.

STUDENTS SHARE THEIR WRITING WITH PARENTS
AT CONFERENCE TIME

Students bring their three strongest pieces to the conference along with the Writing Assessment Scale and the Student Self-Assessment form. They know they're responsible for explaining their writing strengths and what they need to work on. Heather will say to her dad, "I'm beginning to use sentences of different lengths in my writing. Let me read to you from my story about Grandma in the car wash. Listen for how a really short sentence after two long ones is really strong sounding." After she gives a couple of examples of strengths, Heather will explain her weaknesses. "I need to use more showing language in my writing and do less telling. Like, I'll say, 'She was mad,' instead of showing a character turning red, throwing things, and screaming until she's hoarse."

During these conversations I listen, clipboard in hand. I write notes to myself to help plan the next trimester. Some involve the needs of individual students that come out during the conference. I'm also looking for trends; if two-thirds of the class tells their parents they need to work more on showing writing, we'll spend more time on show-don't-tell exercises. In the portion of the parent conference devoted to writing, my goal is to remain silent until the end, at which time I say, "Now we all know what progress Heather has made in her writing and what she needs to work on in the coming trimester. Do you have any questions for her?"

WE CREATE AND USE RUBRICS
FOR INDIVIDUAL ASSIGNMENTS OR GENRES

Oftentimes, the teaching strategies we use are a reflection of our own experiences as students. If one of our teachers did something to motivate or inspire us, we may try to duplicate that strategy or attitude in our own classrooms. Likewise, if we were turned off to some aspect of our schooling, we may try to find strategies to engage our students in ways we weren't. I began using rubrics as a reaction to my own educational experiences in the middle grades. I got an assignment, turned it in, and based on the ratio of red to black ink on my paper, received a grade. I wasn't sure what the grading criteria was before handing in the assignment, just that it had to be "good." When I received the piece back from the teacher, I was mostly interested in the red letter on the upper right-hand corner; if it was good enough not to be grounded, it was good enough for me. I rarely examined the copious red ink liberally spread throughout my assignment.

When I became a teacher, I didn't want to follow the same procedures employed by my middle-grade teachers. First, I wasn't going to write carefully and thoughtfully over each of my students' papers without the certainty of an audience—in other words, work harder on their writing than they did. I care enough to respond to their writing—they better care enough to learn from my responses. Second, I wanted to be sure any student who wanted to excel could. The criteria for excellence had to be made explicit. I looked at my own writing. Letters to friends (and now, e-mail), parent letters, announcements for school and district bulletins, grant proposals, and letters to the editor all had a clear audience, a clear purpose, and clear measure of effectiveness: do I get my message across? I wanted my students to understand that writers must adapt their voice, style, vocabulary, and other variables according to audience, purpose, and genre.

In my first attempts to communicate a sense of writing quality to my students, I distributed a revision guide specific to the genre in which we were writing. By the end of that particular genre study, the revision guide became a grading rubric. I could say, "Get out your piece and examine it in relation to the guidelines in the autobiographical incident revision guide." The rubric had ten qualities; each was graded on a four-point scale. I knew this was a step up from the model that features an all-knowing teacher taking the paper behind the secret curtain, pulling a grade from out of the vapors, and writing a letter from A to F (excluding, for some reason unclear to me, "E") on the corner of the paper. The students could clearly see the criteria being used to evaluate their writing and could revise their work to make it better. Even so, something was still bothering me. I was still the source of knowledge, supplying for them the ladder of success. I wanted them to be able to carve the rungs and assemble their own ladders.

In the last few years, I've begun the study of a genre as described in Chapter 2. We have to immerse ourselves in reading within a genre, carefully study and list the qualities of strong writing on chart paper, try our own idea-gathering and rough drafts, and share our work with peers before we can talk about evaluation. I put the blank Writing Assessment Rubric (see page 126) on the overhead and say, "When you finish a final draft in this genre, what should you be looking for to assess your work?" Looking at our class-generated chart on the bulletin board together, I fill in the blanks on the rubric with the attributes they suggest. We discuss the importance of each attribute and the wording that should go on the rubric. For example, someone might suggest we write, "Uses lots of dialogue."

I (or a student) will ask, "Does a story have to have lots of dialogue to be good?" We'll then discuss the use of dialogue. They'll usually conclude that dialogue can move a story along in an interesting way, but it can also be overdone. Some good stories have very little dialogue ("Beating a Bully" in this collection has one line of dialogue). So, on the rubric we'll write something like, "Good use of dialogue" to leave options open for the writer.

When we've listed enough criteria on the rubric, each one will receive an appropriate value. In the past *I've* weighed the items on the list, giving each a relative point value (a sample completed Writing Assessment Rubric can be found on page 127). After the point values are filled in, I duplicate the rubric for each student. Next time, I'll try to engage the students even more deeply in the process by asking them "Which of these attributes should be worth the most points, and why?" I'll try letting them determine the relative value of each attribute. I think it'll work.

At the end of a unit of genre study, each student hands in a final draft with the class-created rubric as a cover page. The student will have circled a point value in each category, and totaled the points in the right-hand column. The second sheet is the Prove It! page (see page 128). Here the student gives examples to support the evaluation. For example, if Attribute 3 is "Uses more showing than telling writing," the student might say, "For Attribute 3, I would point to page 2, paragraph 1, where I describe my brother's room instead of just saying, 'The room was a mess.'" Students almost always evaluate themselves fairly, and by this point, most of my job is simply to agree with their evaluations.

Writing is still hard work for students, just as it is for us. By allowing students to discover the attributes of quality writing, they see that good writing is not determined by meeting demands sent from some higher power and inscribed on clay tablets, but by the reader's response after carefully gathering evidence from the writing. By giving students time to compose, revise, and discuss their own attempts in a genre, they see that improvement is possible. My students work much harder at writing than I did as a middle-grade student, and at the end of each genre study, they've learned far more than which letter is written in red on the upper right corner of their completed assignment.

The key to student success in academics or behavior is to provide them with good examples. I hope the 25 read-alouds that follow will supply such examples for your students, and that you and they will enjoy the stories.

Autobiographical Incidents

◇ BY TERRY McLAUGHLIN

NAVIGATING THE STRAIGHT AND NARROW

My formative school years were spent sitting ramrod straight, hands folded against mischief, one elbow crooked near that of my partner in a double oak desk—the kind with wells for ink and wrought iron legs that waited to scrape the shins of the clumsy. Sixty girls were packed into each elementary-level room, cowed into a surreal silence by nuns who had escaped Hitler's Germany. Those women drilled us raw recruits in mathematics, language arts, and a pencil-thin interpretation of what was acceptable behavior, their accents hinting of torture and mayhem for anyone who opposed their almighty collective will.

Dad was transferred one winter, and my family traded frigid Washington state for southern California's balmy breezes in the middle of my third-grade year. The ensuing culture shock was based on much more than palm trees, swimming pools, *taquerias,* and even that my new school was coed. The teaching nuns were Irish, and their accents and their classroom management techniques more user friendly. They wore sunglasses and whistles, hiked up their long habits by twisting them in their rosary beads so they could join the flag football games, and drove around at night visiting the sick—delivering the crumbling remains of a cake they'd "tasted" repeatedly in the car on the way over.

My early training earned me the approval of my new teacher, Sister Regina Assumpta. And, in a few weeks, I discovered that my ability to keep my mouth shut, my eyes straight ahead, and my feet quietly on the floor beneath me was worth four A's for conduct on the quarterly report card. Two of the A's had pluses added—little asterisks for excellence.

I stared at those pluses for a long time. They were better than money in the bank, more thrilling than a bobsled careening down the Matterhorn. I was elated. I was greedy. I began plotting for more. Those grades for behavior had been a cinch, so much easier than sweating through math tests or filling in the boring blanks in the spelling workbook. If Sister thought I had been a good kid up to this point—well, just wait.

A few weeks later we filed back into our classroom after the long lunch recess. We slumped at our desks, wilting in the steamy aftermath of nation ball wars fought on a black pavement griddle. Sister Regina Assumpta stood before us, her soft brogue droning an introduction to the latest tale in our readers before she selected a student to read the first paragraph.

I sighed and flipped ahead through the pages, peeking at the faded watercolor illustrations, counting pages. I struggled to keep my eyes open.

Suddenly, there was a blip on my student radar. A suspicious, subtle change had taken place in the normal rustles, shuffles, and murmurs that 20 warm bodies make in a schoolroom. I studied my classmates, noting the spasm of a suffocated laugh, the pursed lips of a smashed smile. Furtive glances were communicating something—but what?

Sister called on Mary Margaret Hanrahan, the girl seated directly in front of me. As she stood to read, Mary Margaret leaned against her desk, nudging it slightly to one side. I shifted uncomfortably, bothered by the sudden untidiness in the row. I heard a pencil

hit the floor behind me and peeked back to see Anthony Bernino shove his desk askew as he reached to pick it up. A tiny squeak across the room—Jim Thompson's desk had slid forward several inches.

The class was on the move. Aisles narrowed, blurred, reformed. Squawks of metal on waxed tile were followed by stifled giggles. Anthony passed me in fitful lurches, like Los Angeles sliding past San Francisco on its seismic track.

Sister's forehead furrowed. Her smiles and words of encouragement seemed hesitant and uncertain. She glanced up repeatedly, trying to catch a culprit in the act, thwarted by a comradery of stealth and angelic expressions.

I sat very still, hands folded across my book, my feet flat on the floor beneath my desk. I tried my best to keep my eyes cast down, fixed on the pages of the reader. As more of my classmates joined the flow, I smugly tallied another plus on the next report card.

I waited for Sister to say something, to stop the tide of blond formica that began to lap around her feet, to note the fact that my desk was still on its mark, but she began a steady retreat. The squeaking, grating, snorting noises increased in tempo; the desks creeping forward en masse. Students who had been banished to the backs of the rows passed me by. I was alone, adrift in a sea of speckled gray linoleum and increasingly uneasy self-righteousness.

No, not alone. Several feet away sat another stranded soul: Hughie Casey. Rubbery lips, plastic crew cut, eyes magnified by the bottle-thick lenses of his glasses, pants missing his ankles by inches, and sunken chest hidden by the kind of navy polyester jacket that was the outerwear of choice for grandfathers at the local country club—Hughie was the class nerd. He looked at me and shrugged. Then he smiled—a shy, slightly conspiratorial smile.

My head snapped forward. There I sat, in my saintly isolation. The female equivalent of Hughie Casey.

Mary Margaret turned and crooked a finger at me, urging me to join the others at the front of the room, where they had Sister circled. But it was too late. There was too much distance to travel, too little time to catch up. And we were nearing the end of the story.

Sister called on Anthony to read the last paragraph, then picked up a ruler and brandished it as the students closest to her threatened to nudge her against the chalkboard. Everyone laughed. "Oh, and aren't you the clever ones?" she asked her captors at story's end. "All that sneaky workin' together. And you two," she tossed her chin at Hughie and me. "I think you may need to straighten those desks a bit."

Sister waved her hands in airy dismissal, and my classmates shifted back into tidy rows, congratulating themselves on a prank well played. I kept my eyes straight ahead, avoiding another stray glance from Hughie Casey, sagging a bit beneath the weight of my halo.

◆ ABOUT THE AUTHOR

Terry McLaughlin has taught writing at all grade levels, from kindergarten to convalescence, and most recently at Humboldt State University and College of the Redwoods. She dreams of writing professionally in addition to coaching her students from the sidelines and hopes that she isn't too lazy—or insecure—to make her dream come true. She loves to revise, or as she says to "tinker with" her writing. She says, "My husband is forever pointing out that if I spent less time tinkering and more time producing new material, I might actually get something accomplished."

◆ NOTES FROM THE AUTHOR

Writing has never been fun for me. I've always been a little in awe of—and a bit suspicious of—those people who keep journals or spout poetry or dash off insightful essays. On the rare occasions that I chose to write something other than a book report or a shopping list, I opted for fiction, hiding my very ordinary self behind characters who had romantic names, wonderful clothes, and who did clever things that were vastly more interesting than anything I had ever attempted. As a result, I reached the age of forty with a lifelong writing portfolio containing only a handful of school assignments, thank you notes, and bits and pieces of dreadful stories that had seemed quite dramatic when I was nine years old.

When I was required to attend a college writing class two years ago, I was horrified to receive an assignment to tell a story about myself. For weeks I poked through dull memories, searching for some incident that I could embellish. As the due date approached, painful insecurities surfaced: My life was boring, nothing in it had any deep meaning, and my writing was inadequate to make sense of whatever I managed to think up. Surely no one would want to read about insignificant characters with saints' names, who wore drab school uniforms and entertained themselves by moving the furniture in a classroom. Even so, I learned something about writing while I suffered through the creation of that essay: There's nothing insignificant about emotions that we all share or about the words on a page that enable a writer and a reader to connect. I'm sure that when I choose to write in the future, my fiction will have a little more of my own, ordinary truths at its heart.

◆ WRITING CHALLENGE: WRITE ABOUT A PERSUASIVE PERSON

Terry McLaughlin ended her story by telling the reader she was "sagging a bit beneath the weight of [her] halo." What do you think she meant by this statement? Earlier in the story she discussed her report card and decided that grades for good behavior were "money in the bank," worth as much to her as a good math or spelling grade, but without all the work. She skillfully showed us that exploiting "good" behavior can lead to unhappy ends. She never told us that; she let us discover it on our own. This is one of many pieces in this collection that shows instead of tells.

Literature, television, and movies are full of characters who use good behavior or false politeness to exploit others. Can you think of some examples? These characters are often called con artists, "con" being short for "confidence." Con artists gain your confidence by being extra nice, and then they take advantage of you. Have you ever conned someone? Have you ever been conned or seen a con artist at work? Have you ever seen a con job backfire, as Terry McLaughlin's did in this story? Try writing about a time when you witnessed a con artist in action.

THE FAN CLUB

◇◇◇◇◇◇◇◇◇◇◇◇◇◇◇◇◇◇◇

Shafts of sunlight cut through the last of the threatening clouds; steam rose from the wet pavement, making the ground look like it was on fire. Outside or in, it didn't matter; the overworked fans delivered no comfort, so I decided to cut through the familiar path that led to the backdoor of my best friend's house. They didn't have air conditioning either, but they had adventure, something I longed for even more than relief from the humidity.

Theresa and her parents had just returned from one of many summer vacations. My family and I never went anywhere. Money? Time? I was never sure which we lacked the most. I only knew it left me searching for a topic to write about when Sister Patricia demanded we describe our summer experiences. I usually settled for some dumb project my brother and I had been persuaded to do around the house. Otherwise, I would have to admit that my only summer getaways were the ones I took vicariously through Theresa's stories. And boy, were they stories!

I always thought she finagled the facts a tad, but I knew that revealing my doubts would also expose my pitiful jealousies of her midyear travels. So I listened, and nodded, and muttered a few "wows" and "ah mans" as Theresa described the cruise ships, the beaches, the airplane rides, and the fancy hotels with elevators you could see through as you rose to the top.

This year they had been to the Bahamas, and Theresa boasted of news that could only be shared out of her mother's hearing range. So we took a walk down the dead-end street. She began telling of this gorgeous fourteen-year-old she had met and how they were going to write each other and all. She swore they had sneaked into a corner and kissed on

the lips! Right on the lips!

We both laughed at the thought of her turning that moment in for the first writing assignment. And, of course, Theresa insisted I cross my heart and hope to die if I told anyone, which I had no problem with because I wouldn't dare share gossip that I didn't even believe myself. So we walked and talked, and she bragged while I dragged through the sticky heat and the sultry tales of a fifth-grade girl's incredulous love affair.

Without warning, Theresa stopped and stooped to pick up what first looked to me like a piece of paper on the ground. "Look!" she exclaimed in her best Broadway voice. "It's a picture of Jesus."

I agreed that it could be called that. The skinny white bearded man with brown hair longer than mine and eyes that seemed to have rolled to the top of his head stood pasted to the clouds that surrounded his bare feet. Both of his hands were stretched out and opened as if he were waiting for something to drop in them. Two half-naked cupids floated on each side, and yellow hues were streaming from the top to the bottom, creating an image of light that was too bright to be real. The thin cardboard that held it all was flecked with dirt and wavy and wrinkled from the rain shower and sun baking it had received that morning. At least one tire track was visible on the squared picture that was stapled to an oversized ice-cream pop stick.

"Let me see that," I asked, and Theresa carefully placed the heavenly scene in my hand. I flipped it to the other side and read aloud, "Dawson Family Funeral Home." The address and phone number were printed beneath in thick, black letters. "It's just a church fan," I told Theresa, and I demonstrated.

The brief breeze it made felt good.

"It's not just a church fan," Theresa insisted as she snatched it back. "It's a picture of Jesus."

"Okay," I conceded. I didn't want to argue.

"Kiss it," she said.

I laughed. I liked it when Theresa made me laugh.

But Theresa did not laugh back. She just stared at me, almost shocked at my defiance of her request. She had stopped walking now, so I stopped, too. And the two of us stood there as close to the middle of the street as you could get.

"Kiss it," she repeated and pushed the fan up close to my face like Father would do with the rounded wafers at Communion.

"No! I'm not kissing that dirty thing." I put my hand over my mouth and the words came out garbled.

"If you love Jesus, you'll kiss it." She held the intruder in place.

I stepped back to allow some space between me, the fan, and Theresa. My tongue began to feel salty as if the tears I was holding back had already fallen.

"I'm not putting my mouth on that picture, Theresa. It's dirty."

"Are you calling Jesus dirty?"

"That's not Jesus!"

"How do you know?"

And I realized I didn't really know, but I was almost certain. So I said, "I just don't see how kissing that picture means I love Jesus."

And then Theresa started shouting.

"You don't know everything. Just because you make all A's and get chosen as the best student each year doesn't mean you know everything. Jesus doesn't care if you're smart or not. Jesus loves everyone."

I felt the tears swimming in my mouth, but they had not hit my face yet. I wouldn't let Theresa see that she could make me cry. I didn't want to win the argument out of pity.

"Then you kiss it," I suggested. My sarcasm gave me strength.

And then right there, right in almost the middle of the street, right above the spot I hoped was mud. Right there on the face of the image of some white man that neither of us would probably ever meet, Theresa took the challenge. She kissed Jesus. And I just stood there. When my mouth opened, all that came out was, "That's nasty."

Theresa smiled as though the angels from the picture had come to rest on her shoulders now, and everything would be all right in her world forever.

"Now you kiss him." She was calmer in her demand this time.

"No," I told her, "I don't believe that's Jesus." But it must have come out like "I don't believe in Jesus" because Theresa backed away from me and gave me a look like I was evil itself.

"You don't believe in Jesus?"

"That's not what I said," I tried to say, but she was back in the pulpit and going on about being saved and telling the nuns and Father. I wanted to grab that stupid fan and slap her silent, but it was too late. She stormed off and ran to her house shouting something about me being a sinner and burning in hell. She took her Jesus with her.

I knew I wouldn't be able to control the tears any longer so I headed back home. Through the shortcut, through the tears, I reassured myself that kissing the picture was a stupid idea, but I felt bad about arguing with my best friend. What had just happened made no sense to me, and I needed to talk to someone. My parents had taught us to pray when confused, but I didn't want to disturb God just then. I figured he was probably a little disappointed in me for making such a big deal over a little picture.

"Jesus," I thought. *"Why couldn't we have found you on a sunnier day in a cleaner place?"*

◇ ABOUT THE AUTHOR

Bernadette Lambert taught sixth grade for seven years, and then became a literacy specialist for Cobb County Schools in Marietta, Georgia. This is her fifth year as a teacher consultant for the Kennesaw Mountain Writing Project. She is a coordinator for a National Endowment for the Humanities grant, Keeping and Creating American Communities. She lives with her husband and two sons in Powder Springs, Georgia.

◇ NOTES FROM THE AUTHOR

When I allow myself to be in a quiet place, both literally and figuratively, I find it easier to remember stories from childhood, and the feelings become easier to retrieve. For this story, I recalled the shock of a friend picking up something from the ground and kissing it. The concern that God was disappointed in me. The doubt of my faith. Yet many of the details remained vague. Perhaps they were irrelevant and did not merit a place within my memory bank.

When I was able to overcome the need to recapture the moment as though it were a photograph, I tackled the story (writing is often a fight, a struggle) as I would any story. I attempted to use words to paint the picture that I wanted to share with my reader. I don't remember if it rained that day. I honestly don't remember if it happened in the summer, but I needed a setting. The one that evolved seemed logical.

I was pleased with some of the images. The steam from the pavement seemed to suggest a bit of mystery, but not in a melodramatic sense. However, I am not sure that the image of the dirty fan— too dirty and disgusting to put to one's mouth—comes through. I am also not as confident in my characterization of the Theresa character.

My favorite part of the story is the last line. It summarizes my real feelings about the incident. What I find amazing, however, is that those feelings did not actually surface until 30 years later. It wasn't until I was able to let go of the need to tell a perfect rendition of the story that I could explore and identify what really happened that day.

◇ WRITING CHALLENGE: WRITE ABOUT A TEST OF FRIENDSHIP

We all want friends and to be part of a group. Sometimes, people play on our need for selfish reasons. As we get older, people exploit this need with more dangerous consequences. For example, exploiting peer pressure to get others to try drugs, join gangs, or hurt others. Have you ever seen anyone ask another person to do something unreasonable as a test of friendship? Has anyone asked this of you? Try writing a story with this theme. Change the names of the characters!

SECOND CHANCE

◇◇◇◇◇◇◇◇◇◇◇◇◇◇◇◇◇◇◇◇

A clear glass and red plastic hummingbird feeder hangs from the eaves outside my kitchen window. Late afternoons, my ten-year-old daughter and I watch the hummingbirds flit across the yard, perch on our feeder, and take long drinks of the nectar we've prepared. Like most of the birds we know, the males are the showy ones—iridescent red head and throat, with a green back and sides giving way to a white chest and belly. The females have just a dainty scarlet bib beneath their chins and are otherwise light and dark shades of olive green. This summer we think we have a nest nearby—two immature birds, the new babies, have also begun feeding. On our side of the glass, we freeze, whispering, watching the family on the feeder. Finally, they fly away. Iris laughs. She says I always cry for two things: mushy scenes in movies and hummingbirds. I tell her I cry whenever I know something beautiful is true. She shakes her head. I think, what does she know? She's ten.

When I was ten, my friends and I played war. There was a perfect slope of grass in our front yard where you could take a hit in the chest and feel the bullet exploding the flesh right out of your back; in slow motion you were lifted up and blown backwards. Hitting the dirt, you'd exhale in an agonized groan, then flop down the hill to lie twitching in some grotesque, contorted position. "Cool," someone would say, and you'd muster enough strength to lift your weapon and pull the trigger in his direction. But those guns and their bullets were made of air, and their damage was always reversible.

My dad kept a gold-triggered Browning automatic shotgun hanging above the entrance to his study. Turns out he bought it when my brother was ten. They used to go hunting in the farm fields near Ithaca. Now and then Dad asks if I remember coming along in the stroller. Of course, I don't. Apparently, he shot at a couple of rabbits, a pheasant or two. But he never hit anything.

On my tenth Christmas there was a pellet gun under the tree for my brother and me. Cooler than a Daisy BB, pellet guns were twice as powerful. It shot one pellet at a time—you pumped it by cracking the barrel when you loaded it. We were supposed to use it under supervision.

Alone after school, I'd pull it out of the closet, unzip the plastic, red flannel-padded case, and go out back, the yellow box of pellets in my hip pocket kachinking like maracas. I'd crack the rifle over my knee, load it, snap it back, and take a position under the old corner oak. Up in the branches, Steller's jays, mourning doves, robins, and squirrels made targets of themselves. I'd aim, take a breath, then let it out slowly and pull the trigger. I got awfully close. But it was some time before I scored my first kill.

The tiny hummer zipped down from above the house, rocketing to a sudden stop at the pomegranate tree. With her delicate black beak and tongue, she probed a large flower, her red-speckled chin floating in and out of the trumpet. Suddenly she backed out, turned, and slid off like a brush stroke for the opposite end of the yard.

I shouldered my weapon, led her generously, then pulled the trigger. She dropped. Incredulous, I ran to where the bird had fallen into my mother's flowers.

The tiny trembling creature revealed an incongruous contusion where the lead pellet had lumped its back out of alignment. A wing buzzed with intensity, then folded. The hummer eyed me from

one side of its head. It flopped over. A dark purple jelly matted the green feathers along her side.

I spoke to the mutilated bird, as if she understood my words, as if my words could fix this unfixable thing. "Oh God, oh God, oh God I'm so sorry," I whimpered. "I'm so sorry I did that to you. I'm so sorry I did that." I was crying, and as I cried, I leaned over and cracked the gun open against my knee, loading another pellet. "I'm so sorry," I said again. "I love you," I said, placing the gray barrel against the hummingbird's small head. I looked away and squeezed. The dull thud. Now there was only half a head, but the bird still flopped in the soft dirt. "I'm so sorry," I repeated, and I loaded up and fired another shot. At last it lay almost still. The claws of her feet trembled. Then they stopped.

Numb, I carefully lifted the still warm, lifeless thing and carried it across the lawn, where I buried it in a hasty grave behind the compost pile. Inside I put the gun away in the closet and lay on my bed, staring at the dots in the light fixture, mortified by my huge, eternal responsibility for the changed world. I stayed in bed after my family came home, sick for the night. Of course, the hummingbird became my secret. But that day was the last I took aim at a living thing.

"You are so funny, Dad," Iris says to me, watching my reaction to these beautiful baby hummingbirds that perch not three feet from us, innocently trusting for their safety. I pull her to me, put my nose in that place behind her ear where the soft, downy hairs tickle, rub my lips in her warm neck. "I love you," I whisper.

"I love you, too," she whispers back.

Outside on the feeder, the hummingbirds rock in the wind.

SECOND CHANCE

◇ ABOUT THE AUTHOR

John Triska teaches third grade at Pacific Union School in Arcata, California. He has taught eighth grade and high school in the past. His students keep nature journals and travel to the Arcata Marsh weekly to follow seasonal changes in vegetation and bird life there. John has two daughters and lives in Arcata. He has been a teacher consultant with the Redwood Writing Project for ten years.

◇ NOTES FROM THE AUTHOR

Life is full of surprises. Who we are today is not necessarily who we will be tomorrow, thanks to our ability to learn and grow. This piece uses irony to compare the narrator as a young boy with the adult person he becomes.

To heighten the irony in my writing, I've been experimenting with a technique known as flashback. Notice how the story begins in the present, flashes back to a time when the narrator was the same age as his daughter, and then returns to the present for the conclusion. Using flashback in this story allowed me to contrast the narrator then and now more effectively than a traditional, linear story line might have.

◇ EDITOR'S NOTE

I have read this story at least ten times. Each time, I am horrified at the part where the hummingbird dies, and in a way, want to stop reading the story right there. The details are so vivid. I think this story is so powerful because John has succeeded in showing the reader the reality of killing. If he had glossed over that part and told us "the hummingbird died," it wouldn't have seemed nearly so tragic. I always have tears in my eyes by the end.

◇ WRITING CHALLENGE: USE FLASHBACK

Try using flashback in a piece of writing. For example, you might remember an experience that ended differently than you had expected it to. Instead of writing the story in the order of events that occurred, try beginning your writing at the end and then flashing back to the beginning. See if you are pleased with the effect.

HOW WE WON THE BEAN FIELD WAR

A certain corner of the world is paradise to every famous naturalist. John Muir had Yosemite. Walden Pond inspired Thoreau. Aldo Leopold wed his soul to the earth at the altar of the Great Plains, the rhythm of the seasons becoming as personal and vital to him as his own heartbeat. I had the bean field.

At some time beans must have grown in the bean field. When I moved to the street adjoining the two-mile-long, half-mile-wide open space enveloped by suburbia, it contained a horse stable, a few ten-foot-deep washed-out gullies, and parched ground in which grew mostly weeds, tumble, and otherwise. A gray-brown liquid (presumably mostly water) of unknown origin flirted constantly with stagnation as it crept between culverts on either end of the field. The railroad track ran lengthwise along the north side of the field, buffering it from Centinela Boulevard.

Though far from pristine, the bean field was my wilderness. I got to read aloud to Mrs. Beard's fifth-grade class my response to The-Most-Beautiful-Thing-I've-Ever-Seen assignment, based on the ring-necked pheasant I encountered in the bean field. The stable workers were friendly and let my buddies and me pet their horses and dalmatians. We impotently fired twenty-five-cent arrows from two-dollar bows at streetwise jackrabbits, who could have eluded smart bombs from stealth jets. Freddy Glick and I built a raft to pole around on the gully sludge while chewing on long weed stems and calling each other "Tom" and "Huck."

The lessons of the bean field were not only those of the great, though smoggy, outdoors, but of human nature as well. Hobos were said to camp in the eucalyptus grove near the tracks, Jimmy Kuhn's big brother had four *Playboy* magazines stashed in the hollowed-out wall of a dry wash, and the bean field was the perfect place to escape all but one of the neighborhood bullies.

Larry Rogers' hilltop backyard bordered the south side of the bean field. From his yard, Larry could see us in all but the most remote corners of our wilderness. We usually managed to spot him before he could yell at us, "Hey, you punks," and zing an arrow over our heads. Later he'd demand his arrow back and slug us if we tried to keep it. On the way home from school, he'd fake like he was going to run us over with his bicycle or tackle us on some nameless suburbanite's well-trimmed lawn and bend or twist a limb in an unnatural direction until we screamed. He usually stopped when we cried.

One summer Saturday, Freddy Glick and I were heading home from our raft trip, covered to mid-thigh with gully mud, and hungry for lunch. Bologna and cheese sandwiches, ours for the making, awaited us at my house. I lived only ten houses down the street from Larry Rogers, but his house stood between our current position and our much-needed rations. Oftentimes, we would spend an extra 20 minutes and go through the trees near the tracks to elude detection by our tormentor, but we were starved, and, after all, we hadn't seen him all day.

We passed below Larry's yard, unheeding of the danger on the hilltop above. "Hey, Punks!" We heard the yell as the rock hit a few feet away. One look up the hill assured us we were still in danger.

Larry had an armful of rocks and was looking to use them. We dove against the cutbank at the base of the hill, crawling quickly, hugging the bank. Larry put more loft on the throws, attempting to land them closer to the bank. We hugged the bank tighter, pressing as much of our bodies against it as we could, inching along toward the spot where the bank rose enough to protect us in a standing position. We had at least a three-minute crawl to get out of his range, and he had plenty of rocks.

"I have an idea," I whispered to Freddy. "Next time one lands close to me, I'm going to pretend like I'm hit. Then we'll make a run for it." I stuck my head up above the bank to give Larry a target and yelled, "You're a lousy shot," then ducked behind the bank where he couldn't see us and crawled backward a few feet. A baseball-sized rock landed inches from the place I had revealed myself (Larry really was a good shot, and I knew it).

Within a second, I crawled forward to the place where the rock had landed and jumped up in full view, hands clutching the top of my head, screaming hysterically. I began to run toward home, Freddy at full speed behind me. I didn't look back, but Freddy told me our attacker was in full retreat toward his own house. We ran along the gully, up to the dead end, and to my backyard without stopping.

Nearly choking on our bologna and cheese every time we mentioned the panic Larry must be feeling, we recounted the story over and over. Finally, Freddy headed for home, careful to walk by Larry's front window to instigate phase two of our now-complete plan.

As soon as Freddy got home, he called me to report our success. "The first thing Larry said was, 'Did he tell his mom?' I told him your head was bleeding really bad, and there was blood all over the bathroom sink and spattered on the floor and we had to get a washcloth all bloody to stop it."

I laughed, "Then what'd he say?"

"He kept saying, 'He didn't tell his mom?'"

"What'd you say?" I asked, still laughing at the terror we had finally returned to its rightful owner.

"I told him your mom was at the store, and we cleaned up the whole bloody mess before she got home. I said we were in the backyard when your mom got home, and she never found out."

"What'd he say to that?"

"He still kept saying, 'His mom doesn't know?' Then he said, 'That's really cool. You guys are really cool.'"

The next day Larry passed Freddy and me on the way home from school. "Hi, guys," he waved from his bike. He never bothered us again.

◇ **ABOUT THE AUTHOR**

Bob Sizoo has taught sixth grade in Eureka, California, since 1986. He is currently on leave from his teaching position to codirect the Redwood Writing Project. He has been a teacher consultant with that National Writing Project site since 1987. He lives in Fieldbrook, California, with his wife, three horses, and two cats.

◇ **NOTES FROM THE AUTHOR**

I spent the first quarter of the story describing the bean field as a place for outdoor play and experiences with nature and worked into the part about encountering the bully. I worried that I spent too much time on the early description, but I wanted to contrast the pleasure and play of the bean field with the danger that Larry added. I still don't know if the description part was too long. What do you think?

◇ **WRITING CHALLENGE: USE DIALOGUE**

Have the students do the worksheet on the next page—"Dialogue Tells It Like It Is." After they complete it, have them compare their "telling" version to the original, and notice whether the story loses some power. You may want to read aloud a couple of versions. Then ask the students to look at a piece of writing they are currently working on and find a section of the piece that would benefit by the addition of dialogue. That's their next writing assignment.

Also try this: In this story, a beautiful setting (at least in the eyes of the protagonist) is the scene of a bully's attack. The opposite can be true as well, a squalid setting can be the scene of a tender love story, or one of hope and renewal. This contrast can add interest to the story. Write about a time in your life where the setting of a story contrasts with its action. Maybe you experienced misfortune or suffering during a birthday or other holiday, or in a beautiful place.

Conversely, maybe you were lost in the woods on a dark moonless night and heard a noise, but it turned out to be a kind stranger who helped you find your way home (Tracy Duckart's story, "Things That Stand Still in the Night" hints at this sort of thing). Describe the setting first, then work your way into the action.

Dialogue Tells It Like It Is

Dialogue can bring your writing to life. The voices of the characters show what they are like and their words can help a story unfold. This usually makes for more interesting reading—better than you, the author, describing what the characters are like and then "telling" the story. As an exercise, read the excerpt below from the ending of Bob Sizoo's "How We Won the Bean Field War." Then revise that part of the story without using dialogue—that is, "tell" the story. Read aloud your version to a partner, listen to your partner's version, and then read aloud the original. Discuss the strengths and weaknesses of each version.

As soon as Freddy got home, he called me to report our success. "The first thing Larry said was, 'Did he tell his mom?' I told him your head was bleeding really bad, and there was blood all over the bathroom sink and spattered on the floor and we had to get a washcloth all bloody to stop it."

I laughed, "Then what'd he say?"

"He kept saying, 'He didn't tell his mom?'"

"What'd you say?" I asked, still laughing at the terror we had finally returned to its rightful owner.

"I told him your mom was at the store, and we cleaned up the whole bloody mess before she got home. I said we were in the backyard when your mom got home and she never found out."

"What'd he say to that?"

"He still kept saying, 'His mom doesn't know?' Then he said, 'That's really cool. You guys are really cool.'"

The next day Larry passed Freddy and me on the way home from school. "Hi, guys," he waved from his bike. He never bothered us again.

THINGS THAT STAND STILL IN THE NIGHT

"Tracy! Shelley! Paul! P–D–B!"

My mother's cheerful voice filled me with dread.

"Tracy, did you hear Mom?" my sister Shelley crooned from our bedroom doorway. "Potty, drinks, and bed!"

I scowled at her over the top of the book I was too distracted to read, feeling the anger welling up from my stomach and into my throat. But I bit it back. I didn't earn my reputation as the good child by voicing every frustration and perceived injustice, as Shelley usually did. I stifled a sigh instead.

"Yes, Shelley, I heard." I clearly enunciated and evenly spaced each word. "I have gone to the bathroom. I have had a drink of water. I am now in bed. I merely want to finish reading this chapter."

"Quit acting like a mother, Tracy. I was just telling you," Shelley scolded as she bounced onto her bed, her Lanz of Salzburg nightgown billowing around her knees.

I ignored her. I hated it when Shelley mimicked Mom, especially when she did it to annoy me, to force me into a response that could get me into trouble. She knew that strategy usually only worked on our younger brother, Paul, but she kept trying it on me. I ducked behind my book, quietly refusing to look up even when Mom swept into the room.

"Are you girls ready for prayers?" Mom asked, straightening the bedspread at the foot of my bed.

I was not ready for prayers. After prayers, Mom turned the lights out. When the lights were out, I went to sleep. And when I slept, I had dreams.

"Mother, would it be alright if I stayed up a lit-tle longer?" I tried not to plead. I tried to sound strong, responsible, adult. "I'd like to finish reading this chapter."

"Tracy, dear, it's eight-thirty, and you have school tomorrow. You know the rules. If I let you stay up, I'd need to let Shelley and Paul stay up." Mom shot me her please-set-a-good-example-for-your-younger-brother-and-sister look. "Besides, aren't you tired, honey? You look exhausted."

I nodded, resigned. Faking a stomachache last night had been equally ineffective.

* * * * * * *

The nightmares started around the same time I abdicated my bedroom to Paul. Since I was the old-est—I would be thirteen in 64 days—I had my own room. But Shelley had just turned eleven (which meant she could stay up as late as I could) when Paul (the youngest) decided he wasn't afraid of the dark anymore. He demanded his own room, argu-ing that he was too old to share his room with a girl. So I stoically, silently, relinquished my most treas-ured privilege.

When I had my own room, my parents used to kneel by my bed to say prayers every night. But as soon as Shelley moved in, Mom and Dad assumed a new position: back by the closet, standing nearer to the foot of my sister's bed than mine, staring at what I imagined was the light of God pouring through the window over our beds and out into the hallway while they recited the bedtime prayer.

I hated sharing Mom and Dad during prayers. I

hated the Andy Gibb and Shawn Cassidy pictures lovingly cut from teen magazines that covered Shelley's side of the room. But most of all I hated sharing a bookshelf with Shelley. My revered Edgar Allen Poe treasury, C. S. Lewis chronicles, and Lewis Carroll's "Alice" books simply did not belong on the same shelf as Shelley's stupid Harlequin romances and Hardy Boys/Nancy Drew mystery stories.

But I didn't hate Shelley, especially after the nightmares started, because every time I flung myself out of the dream, I would have to go to the bathroom—which meant asking for help:

"Shelley," I whispered loudly enough to wake the dead. "Are you awake?"

Shelley rolled over and pulled the covers over her head.

"Shelley, please, please wake up. I have to go potty."

"So go," she groaned through three layers of blankets.

"Will you stay awake until I come back?"

"Sure." I could barely hear her now.

"Shelley, please. This is important. Will you please promise to stay awake until I come back? Shelley?" I knew I was begging, but I accepted then what would have rankled me in the safety of daylight: I needed her.

"Yes," she finally agreed.

"Okay, I'll be right back."

I pushed the covers down, crawled over them to crouch at the foot of the bed, and jumped straight through the doorway onto the hall carpet. I looked both ways, even though the menacing darkness at one end of the hall that was the living room hurried my steps, propelling me toward the insignificant nightlight in the bathroom. I never liked the nightlight that Paul and Shelley insisted upon: It only served to deepen shadows. While I sat on the toilet, I divided my attention between what I hoped wasn't hovering behind the bathroom door and what only kids would believe lurked in the bathtub. I didn't know what was frightening me so terribly, but my imagination supplied a parade of possibilities from the ghost of someone buried alive under the bathtub to my own personal Jabberwocky.

The nightlight also made it harder for me to see on my way back. I had to push my fingertips along the wall so I wouldn't miss the bedroom door. I could almost feel a black cat clawing its way through the plaster, almost hear the heartbeat of a dying old man pounding beneath my feet. I rarely walked back to the bedroom.

"Tracy?"

"It's okay, Shelley," I hushed, breathlessly grateful that she had indeed stayed awake. "It's just me. You can go back to sleep now."

"Tracy, what are you so afraid of all of a sudden?" By now, she had poked her head out of the jumble that was her blankets.

"Nothing." That admission pained me. I knew—deeply, irrevocably—that there was nothing to be afraid of. The fact that I couldn't control my fear shamed me. I wanted to repeat that "Nothing"—I wanted to make it true—but the second time it stuck in my throat.

"Have you told Mom about it?"

"No one need know about this, Shelley. I can deal with it by myself."

"You should talk to Mom about it, Trace."

"Good-night, Shelley."

Shelley mumbled something that could have been good-night, could have been an exasperated growl. But Shelley never mentioned my recent humiliating habit to anyone, not even when she was mad at me.

*   *   *   *   *   *   *

Once again, I shuddered awake. My eyes snapped open. I lay in bed, body rigid, teeth clenched. Only my eyes moved, darting into every dark corner, making sure the nightmare did not follow me into reality. I remained absolutely motionless, knowing—as every child will vehemently attest—that this would make

me absolutely invisible. Then I stifled another shudder: I had to go to the bathroom. I couldn't bear to wake up Shelley yet again, so I clamped my knees together and pulled them to my chest in a desperate attempt to ignore my bladder and go back to sleep, but just then the minute hand on our clock shot forward with such velocity that I almost wet my panties—2:19. It was no good; I had to wake Shelley.

"Shelley?"

"I'm awake."

"Shelley, I have to go potty. Willy —." I sat up. "Oh, my God, Shelley. I remember the dream!"

"Mmmm."

I could feel her slipping back into sleep, so I rushed on.

"Okay. We're living in this same house, only you and Paul aren't born yet, but I'm the same age. Anyway, there's a man in the house, and he's chasing me. I can even see what he looks like; he has blue eyes and blond hair. You'd probably think he's cute."

I felt the terror tug at me again, shortening my breath. I shook my head and continued, trying to dispel the emptiness in those ice blue eyes that still felt so close, so menacing.

"At first I'm not sure why he is in our house, but then I see the knife in his hand. He wants to kill me. I tell Mom and Dad that there's a man trying to kill me, but they won't help. You see, Mom is an alcoholic and Dad is insane. I'm on my own." My eyes shot to the right, realizing a second later that I had seen only Shelley's shadow on the closet door.

"I finally give up on Mom and Dad because I see the killer in the hall, waiting for me. I run all through the house, trying to hide from him, dodging Mom and Dad because they keep getting in my way, and I finally make it to the kitchen, but I trip and fall on my back. Before I can get up or even roll over, the killer comes slowly around the corner. He starts to lean over me, his knife getting closer and closer and closer, but I can't move. Then I wake up. I know there's a lot more in the dream, but I…"

Shelley was asleep. I didn't want to wake her up again, but I wasn't sure I could go to the bathroom when everyone in the whole house was sound asleep. I decided to try. I looked toward the door to make sure the coast was clear—and saw him.

The killer's shadowy figure, much bigger now than in my dream, filled the doorway. His head grazed the top of the door frame, and his shoulders rubbed against both sides of the doorjamb. I froze. The killer stared, motionless. I mentally plunged through my personal store of things-to-do-in-case-of-emergency… without success. I couldn't get to the phone in the kitchen because the killer blocked my only means of escape. If I screamed for help, the killer would get to me before my parents could, and I wasn't sure anymore that they could help. So I sat and the killer stood. Neither one of us moved; neither one of us spoke.

Slowly, I began to feel an angry sort of indignation. It wasn't fair that dream killers could hurt me when I was awake, maybe in places like Narnia and Wonderland, but not in my own bedroom, in my own house. I closed my eyes and shook my head, desperately hoping the killer would just go away.

When I opened my eyes, I saw the killer mocking me, shaking his head in the same rhythm I established, and—and….. I lowered my left arm. The killer lowered his right. I leaned to the right. The killer's head changed shape and floated onto the door. I lay down, and the killer disappeared altogether.

I buried my face in the pillow, fighting tears and listening for Shelley's regular breathing. I let the relieved staccato of my own heart eventually lull me to sleep.

◇ ABOUT THE AUTHOR

Tracy Duckart teaches Freshman English at Humboldt State University and at College of the Redwoods in Humboldt County, California. She has been a teacher consultant with the Redwood Writing Project since 1996. She enjoys cooking and camping and spending time with her animals.

◇ NOTES FROM THE AUTHOR

The conclusion of this story gave me fits. I wanted to avoid the obvious; I wanted to be subtle. I didn't want to just come out and say, "There was no ghost killer: I was staring at my own shadow," but whenever I shared early drafts with my writing group, friends, relatives—whomever I could get to read the story—I got the same questions. What happens to the killer? What happens at the end? Is the killer real?

Because I wanted readers to recognize rather than read that I was terrorized by a shape I created myself, I had to provide some clues. I had to reveal how I could cast that shadow, so I made a reference to "what I imagined was the light of God pouring through the window over our beds and out into the hallway." When some fresh readers still admitted confusion, I knew I had to offer a reminder in the last third of the story—"My eyes shot to the right, realizing a second later that I had seen only Shelley's shadow on the closet door"—in the hopes that repetition and proximity would prove sufficient. Do you think they did?

◇ EDITOR'S NOTE

Tracy Duckart's piece has a lot in common with some of the other fine stories in this collection. Her reflection above attests to her struggle with showing the readers about the shadow without telling them. She also uses a lot of dialogue to tell the story.

I like the way she describes the conflict she has with her sister contrasted with Shelley's sensitivity to her fear. Even though they argued all the time, Shelly never used Tracy's fear against her.

◇ WRITING CHALLENGE: WRITE ABOUT A CONFLICT WITH SOMEONE YOU CARE ABOUT

Sometimes siblings or friends will fight and argue all the time. Even so, if one ever really gets in trouble, the other usually comes to the rescue. Does this happen with your brothers, sisters, or in families you know? How about with your friends? Try writing about a relationship you've been a part of or witnessed in which two people seem to be in conflict, but really care about and stand up for each other when the chips are down.

NEW SHOES

◇◇◇◇◇◇◇◇◇◇◇◇◇◇◇◇◇◇◇◇◇

I was not one of those girls who was always getting into trouble. Occasionally, my teachers would write, "Gerry talks too much" or "Gerry is a bit too social." But, basically, I was a good kid. I never intentionally hurt anyone or destroyed anything—not until the day of the shoe, that is. And really, then, I was just trying to show off and impress my friend. I didn't think I was doing anything wrong. Even at the age of five, I knew the value of money, and I knew that new shoes were special.

I loved new shoes. Besides this pair, I remember one other pair of shoes on my pudgy little feet. They were white sandal-like T-straps. They were the kind of shoes that had holes stamped in the toes. Not the kind that makes your toes stick out, but the kind that made a symmetrical pattern across the front. I would practice buckling and unbuckling those shoes until little lines and creases were worn into the straps. I can still remember looking down and seeing my chubby feet bulging out around the double straps. The real shoes, though, the ones about which I write, were the very first shoes I ever had that didn't lace, buckle, or tie. I could just slip them on and slip them off! They were genuine ox-blood Cambridge penny loafers. I learned this fancy name later. I just called them "the kind of shoes you put pennies in that don't lace, buckle, or tie." I don't remember where I got them or how I got them. I just remember that wonderful, exciting feeling of new shoes, and I couldn't wait to wear them to school.

The next morning I met Bobby Cookson on the corner as usual. We always walked together along the path through Carson Park. Bobby called it the shortcut. It must have been spring. It was a sunny day and the shrubs and bushes along the way were flush with leaves and flowers. Rhododendrons may even have been in bloom.

"Bobby, look at my new shoes," I said, almost immediately as we started across the path. "They don't buckle, and they don't tie. Look at the pennies. Do you want to touch them?" Before he could answer, I had the shoe off and in his hand. I hopped along on one foot getting just the tip of my white sock dirty while he took a good look at the penny in my shoe.

Almost as fast as I had handed it to him, I grabbed it back saying, "Here, give it back to me, I'll show you what I can do." Wiping the dirt off my sock, I put the shoe back on my foot. "Wanna see how far I can kick it?" I asked. Again I didn't wait for an answer.

The next part I remember in slow motion. I can still vividly see myself in full animation; raring back and kicking that right shoe into the air—higher, higher, and higher. Then very slowly watching it come down, down, down and land in the bushes.

We never found that shoe again. Bobby went on to kindergarten without me. I, on the other hand, was in big trouble.

◇ **ABOUT THE AUTHOR**

Gerry Tollefson teaches second grade at Lincoln School in Eureka, California. She has lived in California, Washington state, and on Long Island in New York. She has two daughters and a son and likes books, movies, jazz festivals, and exploring new places. Gerry has been a teacher consultant with the Redwood Writing Project since 1991.

◇ **NOTES FROM THE AUTHOR**

I still live in the same town I lived in when I was five, so I often drive by the park where I kicked off my shoe. I'd thought about this incident many times in my growing up years and laughed or chuckled at the vision it created in my mind. Sometimes I even winced a little.

In the summer of 1991 I was part of the Redwood Writing Project's Summer Institute. One of my assignments was to write an autobiographical incident. The due date was always in the back of my mind, nagging at me, but still no stories from my life seemed worth writing about. While visiting my mother and brother in the Bay Area that August, we went to an Oakland A's baseball game. There, in the middle of the game, it hit me: I would write about losing my shoe. I don't know what triggered the idea—maybe it was being with my family—but anyway, I was so excited, I took out my tablet and started then and there. I wrote and wrote. Sunshine, baseball, popcorn, beer, and I'm writing an autobiographical incident.

◇ **EDITOR'S NOTE**

I can just see Gerry at the ballgame writing in her notebook surrounded by cheering fans. Most writers have some way of recording ideas and observations that occur to them. My friend in Oregon, Kim Stafford, always carries a pocket notebook when he travels to record what he calls, "local knowledge." Some people keep a notebook next to the bed to record those flashes of inspiration that bubble up into consciousness in the middle of the night. Others carry around a pocket tape recorder so they can record thoughts even while driving, in low-light conditions, or when writing would be otherwise difficult. I usually have a spiral-bound notebook within reach. One thing we all know: when those observations and ideas come, if we don't record them, we'll likely never get them back.

◇ **WRITING CHALLENGE: WRITE ABOUT AN EVENT THAT LED TO TROUBLE**

Sometimes when we get into trouble, it's no surprise. We know all along that what we're doing will get us into hot water. Other times, we get in trouble for something that seems harmless in the instant we do it, but then, given a moment to think about it, we see where it's heading—toward trouble. Gerry Tollefson's story is a good example of the latter. As we read the story, we know that Gerry kicking her brand new shoe into the air in an area of thick shrubbery is just asking for trouble. We also know that she loved her new shoes and wouldn't risk losing one intentionally. Nevertheless, she did lose one.

Have you ever been in a situation in which you did something you didn't think at the time could lead to trouble, but did? Try writing about that situation.

THE BASEBALL DOLLAR

❖◇❖◇❖◇❖◇❖◇❖◇❖◇❖◇❖

Duke Snider, Maury Wills, Gill Hodges, and the rest of the Dodgers packed their bags in Brooklyn and came to L.A. I was eight years old. I knew a little about baseball, but most of my knowledge came from my Chicago-born grandma, who claimed to have been at the World Series game where Babe Ruth pointed to the fence and smacked one out against her beloved Cubs "at the exact spot he had pointed to." She was already a Dodgers fan when she and Grandpa moved to L.A. because, as she informed me, "Cubs fans need a back-up team to cheer for." The famed Babe Ruth incident happened 35 years earlier, and the Cubs haven't returned to the series to this day, so I guess she had a point. Beginning in 1958 we both had a home team to cheer for.

"Deuces are wild," Vin Skully would announce over the cream-colored Bakelite radio that sat on the painted table next to my bed. "Two balls, two strikes, two on, two out, and the flame-throwing right-hander stares at Roseboro for the sign. Matthews steps out of the box. A dead-pull fastball hitter, Eddie knows this is strength against strength. He steps back up to the plate. Drysdale shakes off a sign and checks the runner at second. Here's the windup and the pitch…" In the six months following the Dodgers' arrival, I learned every player in the National League, and, thanks to Vin Skully's colorful narration, could picture every stadium in the country. If I had spent as much time studying as I did listening to baseball, I'd be skipping two grades in the fall.

In those days I got a nickel a week allowance. A nickel could buy a Hershey bar or five pieces of Bazooka or Double Bubble; I usually spent my five cents on one of those options at the little green store on Normandy on the way home from Raymond Avenue school. My dad always told me I was a wastrel, lecturing about my allowance "burning a hole in my pocket." He had a pamphlet from an investment company explaining that if you had put a penny into the bank around the fall of the Roman Empire you now would have millions of dollars through *the magic of compound interest.* Somehow putting my allowance in the bank every week so I could afford a bicycle when I turned sixty didn't much appeal to me.

Then I got the dollar. I didn't exactly steal it, but it wasn't a gift blowing in the wind, either.

During the Dodger's second season in L.A., Ed, my dad's buddy from work, invited the two of us to go to the Saturday ball game. The baseball fantasy that crackled into my bedroom every night was about to come to life. The Pirates were coming to town. That meant that not only could I see all the great Dodgers, but also Bill Mazeroski, Dick Groat, and the budding superstar Roberto Clemente were going to be on the field playing against them. All in front of my very eyes. My prayers had been answered.

I stayed up late listening to the Friday night game. I listened to the entire post-game show, and Polka Parade after that. I couldn't sleep. By the time we left the next morning, I had eaten breakfast, oiled my two-dollar glove, talked my dad into playing catch in the front yard for a few minutes, and sat on the front porch pounding a baseball into my glove to shape the pocket perfectly for the foul ball that I hoped would come my way that afternoon.

"The light at the end of the tunnel" is a cliché for perseverance rewarded. But cliché became real, walking through the stadium tunnel that day as the tiny view of the stands on the opposite side of the

L.A. Coliseum slowly grew larger and larger until, upon reaching the end, the whole stadium and field spread out before us. Never had I seen such a huge, green lawn. Groundskeepers wheeled their striping machines, leaving neat chalk lines from home plate all the way to the outfield fences. Others raked the infield to perfection. Another brought out the clean, white bases to attach to their respective spots on the field, soon to become hubs of activity. Fans filed in every tunnel. "We're in row 42, seats 23, 24, and 25," Ed instructed.

"Great seats," my dad commented, shuffling down the row. As I lowered into the wooden seat, only glancing away from the field long enough to check the 24 painted on the backrest, I couldn't imagine any seat in this massive stadium that wouldn't be great. Dad and Ed settled on either side of me.

The players sauntered onto the field. I was impressed by their casualness, expecting to see them goose-stepping onto the field, chests puffed out, eyes narrowed, and completely focused on the solemn task before them. But they were talking and joking and casually beginning to toss the ball back and forth just like we did at the Little League Park. Doesn't he know he's Duke Snider? I thought. Hey, that's Sandy Koufax talking to Don Drysdale, just like my dad discussing the weather with Uncle George. Don't they know who they are?

After warming up the players gathered outside their respective dugouts, then lined up along the baselines for the national anthem. Ed, Dad, and I stood at our seats, caps over our hearts, listening respectfully. Finally, the umpire yelled, "Play ball!"

During the first inning Dad handed out the waxed paper-wrapped bologna and cheese sandwiches. Mine could have been filled with peanut butter and mud, for all the attention I paid it. Don Drysdale was on the mound. Who could pay attention to food? I think Dad felt the same way. He had passed out Mom's sandwiches motivated by some subconscious paternal obligation to provide for his offspring; his attention was riveted to the pitching mound just as powerfully as mine was.

By the top of the seventh inning, the relentless barking of the food vendors had triggered some primal need for sustenance. "Let's get some peanuts," implored Ed.

"Good idea," replied Dad.

"Hey, peanuts!" Ed yelled to the vendor climbing the stairs in the aisle next to him. "Three bags, please." The crack of the bat on a Drysdale fastball stirred the crowd. Dick Groat had led off the inning with a line drive single over Maury Wills; until then, the Pirates had managed only one hit in six innings. Drysdale was still throwing good heat, but the Dodger bats had quieted since the two-run first inning, and a two-run lead is never safe with any pitcher.

"Seventy-five cents," said the peanut man, apparently unfazed that he could ask so much money for only three bags of peanuts. Bill Mazeroski stepped up to the plate. The fearsome Roberto Clemente strode into the on-deck circle. Ed glanced away from the game long enough to hand the peanut man a dollar.

"Steeerike!" yelled the umpire as Drysdale's pitch smacked into Johnny Roseboro's glove. The crowd roared.

"Here's your change," said the peanut man, handing Ed a quarter, as Drysdale wound up for his next pitch.

"Ball one," the umpire signified with a nod of his head and a sideways jab of his left index finger. The crowd quieted. Ed leaned away from me and slipped the quarter into his pocket, his gaze never leaving the field. Drysdale shook off a sign from Roseboro, nodded, and straightened on the mound. He wound up and smoked a heater toward the plate. He wasn't tiring; that baby sizzled. But Mazeroski was looking fastball, and stroked a liner over the pitcher's head before he could even get his glove arm extended. The crowd grew tense. Roberto Clemente, the young superstar with fire in his fists and fame in his future approached the plate. He

stepped into the box, and pawed at the dirt like a bull ready to charge.

Every eye in the stadium honed in on the white ball in the pitcher's right hand. Even the vendors ignored their trays of Cokes and Cracker Jacks, to contribute to the crowd's anxiety. Drysdale checked the runners and zinged a fastball low and tight, slipping under Clemente's powerful swing. "Steeerike!" the umpire yelled even more dramatically, apparently sensing the 40,000 eyes upon him.

My dad reached into his pocket and pulled out a dollar. "Give this to Ed," he said, handing me the bill without looking away from the game. He wanted to reimburse Ed for the peanuts.

"Here," I said tapping Ed on the shoulder.

Ed looked briefly at the bill and waved his upturned hand at me saying, "No, no, no." His eyes were fixed on the pitcher by the time he got to the third "No." Drysdale checked the sign; Clemente stepped out of the box.

I turned back to Dad. "Ed doesn't want it," I told the side of his head. He cocked his head slightly toward me and, still riveted to the pitcher, said, "Give it to Ed."

Rotating toward Ed, I made another attempt to give him the dollar. Drysdale went into his stretch. "No, no, no," Ed waved the money away. I could have been handing either one of these men a gold ingot or a live grenade and would have gotten the same response. I looked at the fortune between my fingers. Both men had refused it twice. I didn't want to nag. And yet, there it was, still in my hand—20 weeks income. If they didn't want it, I knew someone who did. I slipped the dollar into my pocket. I tried to pay attention to the rest of the game, but I couldn't stop thinking about that hot fortune pounding against my right thigh. Maybe it really would burn a hole. I think the Dodgers won.

* * * * * * *

For a week I was rich. Monday I treated Tyrone Biggs to an Abba Zabba. On Tuesday M&Ms and Necco Wafers rained down on Danny and J.D. Bubblegum all around on Wednesday, and a fistful of penny candies on Thursday left me with a dime by Friday morning. My dad was right; the fortune a wise investor would have parlayed into an early retirement, I had used to infect a neighborhood with dental cavities. I might as well spend this last dime on the way home from school, I thought during multiplication drills on Friday. After all, I've done all my chores this week, and I'll get another nickel tomorrow for my allowance.

By 3:10 P.M. the dime was gone, and the owner of the little green store was ten cents richer. I walked home and into the kitchen where Mom was pushing together the Friday night meat loaf. I blew a respectable bubble and said, "Hi, Mom."

"Hi," Mom replied. "You've sure been chewing a lot of gum lately." Before I could craft an acceptable reply, she continued, "Oh, that reminds me—did Dad mention that dollar from the baseball game?" Again, without allowing time for an answer, she went on, "We decided to call that your allowance for the next twenty weeks. I hope you haven't spent any of it yet. Here, come over here and look where we marked the calendar. We marked each of the next twenty Saturdays with an 'X'." She began to flip through month after month. "See, you'll get your next allowance on January sixth."

◇ ABOUT THE AUTHOR

Bob Sizoo has taught sixth grade in Eureka, California, since 1986. He is currently on leave from his teaching position to codirect the Redwood Writing Project. He has been a teacher consultant with that National Writing Project site since 1987. He lives in Fieldbrook, California, with his wife, three horses, and two cats.

◇ NOTES FROM THE AUTHOR

Have you ever gotten something you wanted really badly, and then found out later it's not as important as you thought? It's happened to me quite a bit. This story is about one of those times. I thought baseball was the entire world, but once I had that enormous sum of money in my pocket, I couldn't think of anything else. One of the members of my writing group said he was disappointed in the story—that he wanted to know more about how the game ended. After all, I had put so much detail in leading up to the climax of the game he felt like he was left hanging. I did that on purpose—I wanted to show the reader how important baseball was to me, so I could show that the dollar must really be important to distract me from the game. I chose to do it my way instead of following the advice of my friend. As a reader/listener, do you think this technique worked?

◇ WRITING CHALLENGE: WRITE ABOUT A CHARACTER'S SHIFTING MOTIVATION

1. Read aloud a piece of your writing to a partner or to your writing group. Write down every comment and suggestion they make about your work. Choose one suggestion you don't want to follow and explain why you want to keep your writing the way it is. Choose another suggestion you do want to follow, and revise your piece. Explain why it's better after following your partner's advice.

2. Try writing a story that begins with one thing being really important to the main character and then shift the focus so that something else becomes even more important.

SOMEBODY'S FOOL

◇◇◇◇◇◇◇◇◇◇◇◇◇◇◇◇◇◇

I hated thirteen! Not only was I the youngest kid in eighth grade, but I believed I was the ugliest and most unpopular—although my best friend, Cheryl, argued she held that dubious distinction. Worse yet, Mom was taking my adolescence even worse than I was. She started saying stupid things like, "Someday somebody will love you for your brains and because you are nice. Remember, there's a lid for every pot. Just wait until you grow up; you'll find people just like you—concerned with the important things in life."

She just didn't get it! I wasn't uninterested, just unsuccessful at being cool. I was well-versed in rock-and-roll stars and knew the words to all the songs on the Top 40 radio station. Besides, I didn't want to be loved for "what was inside." I wanted to be desired for my outward appearance just like all of my peers. I hungered to be worshiped for my perfect hairdo, pimple-free skin, and fashionable clothes. I wanted to hear gasps of excitement when the bottle spun toward me at parties. And I craved desperately to be noticed by Kenny Campbell.

Kenny was every thirteen-year-old girl's dream. Even some of the fourteen-year-olds liked him. Rumor had it a ninth grader was intending to ask him to the Sadie Hawkins' Dance! Kenny had perfect hair, the bluest eyes, was the tallest boy in the class, and had the nerve and creativity to steal the substitute teacher's purse and return it with a sample bottle of whiskey inside to get her in trouble. Kenny was number one in my book, even if he couldn't spell or do long division or pass the history test. Kenny was every movie star and teenage singer rolled into one. He could hit, run, make touchdowns, become elected student council president, and even the teachers loved him because he was "all boy." I would have killed to win Kenny's approval, though I'm not sure even that would have attracted his attention.

My mother could not understand my obsession for someone who seemed to her to be so ordinary. "One of these days you will see," she would say. "The fire that burns brightest burns out first." She would have loved for me to forget my silly infatuation and to have gone to the sock hop with Arnold Tropfeld, the only boy in our entire junior high who could use a slide rule.

* * * * * * *

I will never forget my surprise and pain the day my best friend, Cheryl, who had braces, thick glasses with rhinestones, and limp, brown hair, showed me the note she had found in her locker.

Roses are red, vilets are blue, your sure cute, and I am to.
A secret admirer. K.C.

No. It couldn't be. Bad enough Kenny wouldn't look at me twice but to send a note to shy, bookwormy Cheryl was unbelievable. "I bet this is a trick," I told Cheryl. "I bet Linda did this to get even for that secret you spread about her and Clarence Trimble."

"We'll see," retorted Cheryl. "I saw him looking at me the other day in music class. Last month in *Seventeen Magazine* I read if you stand tall and believe in yourself, others will believe in you, too. I've been believing I'm popular all week and already it's working! I bet he's going to ask me to go to the school carnival with him."

 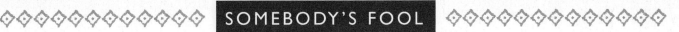

My mother had been reassuring Cheryl that once her braces were off, her skin cleared up, she was old enough to get contacts, and she had "grown into herself," she would be a beauty. Maybe Kenny Campbell could see her potential and wanted to get his bid in early. I was heartsick and jealous like I had never been before—not even when Edith Spurd got her own horse.

I tried to tell myself I didn't care anyway about a boy who wore mirrors on his shoes to get a laugh. Or who called Ramona Brindle "cootie" to be mean and get a snicker out of the other boys; how could I justify my fascination with someone who could be so cruel to others? But the facts remained, I was undercut by Cheryl because she had faith, and Kenny still hadn't noticed I was alive. Maybe I did need to read that article in *Seventeen Magazine*.

Two weeks later when I met Cheryl at our usual after-school meeting place, I was prepared for the daily litany of K.C. stories. How he passed her three notes in history class. How he opened his mouth full of mashed potatoes in the school cafeteria and honored her with the game of "See." How he had three of his friends call her and inquire whom she liked. Friday was the school carnival, and we both figured Kenny would ask Cheryl to go with him. Not only would my best friend be going to the fair with Kenny, but I wouldn't have anyone to go with myself. I went to the library on my way home from school and checked out three books to read over the weekend.

* * * * * * *

The next morning in the hall after math class, Cheryl looked up at me with tears in her eyes. "I'm never coming back to this crummy school ever again," she said in a quavering voice. She handed me a note. I read:

April fools! You just won the ugliest girl in the school contest. The prize is this note for your scrapbook. Come back in 20 years after you take some beauty pills.
K.C.

"He gave it to me in front of all his friends," sobbed Cheryl. "They just laughed. What did I ever do to them? How can I face school on Monday?"

I was dumbfounded and disgusted. Even more shocking were the words coming from my lips—they were my mother's!

"Don't worry," I said. "Someday somebody will love you for your brains and because you are nice. Remember Cheryl, there's a lid for every pot. Just wait until you get older; you'll find other people just like you who are concerned with the important things in life."

Cheryl just looked at me, disbelieving.

"Cheryl, he's just a dumb boy," I said, starting to cry. "No one will even remember him after junior high school. Someday, no one will laugh at his stupid jokes and disgusting grin. Remember, a hot fire burns out fast!"

"Don't you know anything?" Cheryl said sharply. "There will always be Kenny Campbells in the world and people who laugh at their stupid jokes just to be popular."

Then Cheryl took a deep breath and drew herself up tall. Behind her glasses, her eyes shone. She reached into her book bag and pulled out a dog-eared magazine. "Go read *Seventeen*," she ordered through a thin smile. "I'll meet you at the corner near my house at 6:00 and we'll go to the carnival together. Think you can get up the nerve to go on the Ferris wheel?"

◆ ABOUT THE AUTHOR

Susan Bennett teaches English at Humboldt State University. She taught junior high English in La Puente, California, before returning to Berkeley for her Ph.D.. Susan has two daughters and lives near Eureka, California, with chickens, ducks, a goat, and a couple of horses. She is the director of the Redwood Writing Project.

◆ NOTES FROM THE AUTHOR

This story is based on a true account, but it didn't actually happen to me. I wrote this story after overhearing a woman tell someone about an experience her daughter had in junior high school. At the time, I also had a daughter in junior high, and I got to thinking how this could have happened to me or my own child. I started to imagine how I would have felt if I had been given the note or if a boy I admired liked my best friend. I considered how terrible I would feel if my daughter had this happen to her. I was mad at this boy I didn't even know.

Not long after overhearing the conversation, I met an adult who reminded me of the kind of person Kenny Campbell might be when he grew up. Then I was able to write the story because I had a real person in my mind to make Kenny come alive to me. I patterned the two girls after myself, my best friend in high school, and my daughter and all her friends put together. In real life none of the characters exist but are composites of many people. I think most writers get their characters this way, from observing how people think, act, look, and sound, then picking and choosing attributes from many to draw pictures of characters.

This story took me four weeks to write with many changes. I read it aloud to people I trusted; I asked my own teenagers if it made sense, and I revised it about five times taking into account many suggestions.

Throughout the revision process, I aimed to write a story that prompted readers to think: Why did Kenny and the boys play the prank? Do you think they wanted Cheryl to feel bad? Why? What did they have against her? Why do you think people behave like Kenny and his friends? Why are certain kids picked on more than others? Why do you think kids like Kenny are sometimes popular? Why do the other kids admire this kind of cruel behavior? If I get my readers to think about these important questions and ideas, then I consider myself having written a successful story.

◆ EDITOR'S NOTE

This story reminds me that sometimes our words or actions have a much stronger effect on people than we realize at the time. Unfortunately, we don't learn about it until much later—after the damage has been done. I wonder if Kenny even remembers this event that meant so much to Cheryl. If so, has he changed? Does he feel remorse for hurting Cheryl? Maybe he's still a self-centered jerk who remembers and thinks, "I don't care; she was ugly anyway."

The story also causes me to wonder about my own school years. Did I, in an attempt to get a laugh from some of my friends, cause any of my classmates this kind of pain? For that matter, did I inadvertently hurt someone's feelings last month or last week or last night? I like this story because it makes me think.

◇ WRITING CHALLENGE: DEVELOP A CHARACTER THROUGH DIALOGUE

Much of this story is told through dialogue. Try writing about someone you know or make up a character based on a combination of people you have known. Think about ways you can show your reader through dialogue what this person is like. As you are deciding what details to include about this person, think about what you want your readers to know and feel about this character. For instance, do you want the reader to like, admire, respect, or be revolted by this person? Try to be subtle, suggesting qualities about your character instead of outright saying them. For example, if your character is a slob, don't have her mother say, "You're a slob." Instead, have her say, "Do you think your friends admire the gravy on you shirt?"

Answer the following about your character:

1. How does the character speak in different situations? Write an example of your character's conversation with his/her:
   - mother
   - brother or sister
   - secret love
   - best friend
   - teacher
   - dentist
   - dog

2. How would the following characters describe your character when she/he isn't around?
   - a parent
   - a teacher
   - a rival
   - a best friend
   - the coolest person in school
   - the most intelligent person in school
   - his/her pet

Also try this: Susan's story is about courage, and explores an interesting theme: how a "bad" or unkind person could bring out good qualities in another. Cheryl didn't let Kenny and his friends ruin her. Sometimes we demonstrate courage by performing heroic, dramatic acts, but more often we show courage simply by continuing on. The characters in this story show their courage or lack of courage in everyday ways. Try writing about a character who shows courage in everyday ways.

◇ BY JOHN TRISKA

SWEET

◇◇◇◇◇◇◇◇◇◇◇◇◇◇◇◇◇◇◇

Gina Lucci was my idea of the perfect sixth-grade girl: tall, brunette, and aloof. Best of all, she was Italian, so of course I loved her. Gina Lucci, Gina Lucci, I would breathe her name in and out as I walked to school each morning, imagining her eyes looking back at me, visualizing her walking with me in the field at school.

"I'm Italian, too," I'd tell her.

"Really?" she'd murmur, and I would say, "Sure. Burastero is my mother's maiden name. My grandmother calls me Giovanni."

Gina would smile and take my hand, and we'd keep walking out in that field.

The truth is, I was terrified to speak with her. Gina would lean up against the ball wall with her two best friends, her hands in the pockets of her short-sleeved jumper, rocking on her heels, staring out over our heads as if she was watching waves roll in on some Mediterranean beach, as if my buddies and I messing around on the field weren't there at all. She exuded independence. That's what made the results of our meeting such a surprise.

Thursday at lunch recess, Dave Frazell had finally had enough of my mooning over Gina. He grabbed me by the back of my shirt and shoved me into the hallway, practically into her as she and her girlfriends walked toward the girls' bathroom.

"John has something to ask you," he blurted, and gave me a final push and was gone. I thought I was going to be sick, but I was thrilled just the same. This was it.

Gina shrugged at her friends. Jane took Cindy by the arm and they left, giggling.

Then Gina raised her eyebrows over those big green eyes, and I knew this was the way it was supposed to be.

"Do you want to go steady?" I asked. I didn't like the sound of my voice. It kind of cracked halfway through the sentence. I wondered if it sounded like that to her, too.

"I've been waiting for you to ask me," she said. What? This seemed unbelievable.

"So you do?" I said flatly, trying to control my pitch. It sounded more like a confirmation than a request. I waited.

"Okay," she said. She looked over her shoulder at her friends who fell over each other in hysterics.

"Then it's settled," I said. "Bye!" I turned and bolted for the field, where Dave and the guys were tripping each other, calling each other wussies. They took me back with slaps on the shoulder. Casually scanning the playground, I spotted Gina and the girls in a huddle by the bathrooms. I wondered what she was telling them.

That afternoon I walked home with Sandy, my next door neighbor. "Of course, you and I could never go steady," I assured her, "since we're neighbors and all."

"Gross. No way," she said. "Anyway, now you have to give her a Christopher." I knew about this. I'd have to act fast and buy a St. Christopher medallion like the ones they sold at McQuarry's Drug Store. They gave them out at church when you were confirmed, but I wouldn't get mine until spring, and here it was October. I planned to ride my bike up there this afternoon and buy one—the dime-sized one with the green enamel trim around it, to go with Gina's beautiful eyes.

"Are you going to kiss her?" Sandy asked me. She stopped and watched me.

I thought about it. "What do you think? Am I supposed to?"

She shrugged. "I don't know," she said, starting up the hill. I hated that about girls. Why couldn't they just tell you what you needed to know?

That night I carefully wrapped the St. Christopher and chain in the box they'd given me at the drugstore. I had to spread out a cotton ball to fit inside the box so the medallion would look just right. Then I made at least ten drafts of the note before I wrote it on the little card I'd bought.

"Dear Gina, for you on this great occasion." No way. Too formal.

"To Gina, who I love." Nope. Too serious. And too short. I didn't want her to think I didn't know what to say.

"To Gina, for going steady with me." That sounded like I was paying her to be with me.

I wanted her to know that I liked her a lot, and that I respected her. And something about our destiny, being Italians, together. I had it!

"*Ciao,* Gina," I began. "You are the one for me. I think you are—" and I searched for just the right word, finally deciding she was sweet, like candy.

Normally I dreaded Fridays. Miss Campbell kept kids after school when they failed a test. She made us study right there in front of her while she graded papers, and when we were ready, we could take the test again, but we had to pass it before going home. I stayed after school every Friday all year, because Friday afternoon was when we took our spelling tests. It didn't matter how much time I spent studying at home. The next day I'd go blank. Miss Campbell was nice about it, really. She never made me feel stupid or anything. She just told me I had to get better at spelling, "one way or another."

"Whether we like it or not," she'd say, handing me a blank sheet of paper to try again, "people judge us by impressions. And the first impression we make when we write is how well we spell."

But this Friday morning I wasn't even thinking about the test. I carried the box with the St. Christopher, and the note tucked into the ribbon, in my lunch bag. I didn't want anyone to see it, because I didn't want anyone to force my moment. I wanted to be alone with Gina when she opened it, so I could see her reaction.

After grammar we had library. I knew I could find a way to be alone with Gina in the book stacks, and if not, right after library was recess. The way my heart was racing, I knew I had to give it to her by recess, or I'd never survive the day. Can a twelve-year-old have a heart attack, I wondered?

When we lined up for library I reached for my lunch above the coat closet. My bag had a hole in it—my pear was squished—and the box fell to the floor right next to Jane Macey. I picked it up quickly and shoved it into my jeans pocket, but it was too late. Jane was whispering to Cindy, and Cindy grabbed Gina by the arm, and by the time I got in the back of the line, it was over. She knew, and they knew, and half the class was going to know by the time we got to the library. I felt myself beginning to panic.

In the hall Gina, Jane, and Cindy stopped at the drinking fountain and leaned over it, running the water and giggling until I came up. They cut in front of me, and Gina got pushed to the back, and there we were.

"Here," I said, handing her the box. "It's kind of crumpled. Sorry."

"Hmm," she said, and then smiled, and ran to catch up with the line. I walked the rest of the way, hoping my heartbeat didn't show through my T-shirt.

We had to sit through a ten-minute lecture on the Dewey Decimal System, and Dave Frazell kept looking at me, then at the girls, then back at me. All I could do was shake my head at him. I felt hot.

Finally free to get up and look at books, I slipped into the closest stack, 921, biographies. From a break in the books, I looked across the library to the round tables, where all the girls in the class were crowded around Gina. She was unwrapping the box. A few of them reached over and held the medallion before I saw Gina looking at it closely. Was she smiling? They were all in the way.

Then she began on the envelope. Oh God, please no! Not here in front of everybody!

She opened the card and read. She definitely smiled! But then Jane grabbed the note from her and read it aloud, and suddenly all the girls were laughing and Cindy was pointing at Gina. My face burning, I turned and opened a book about Louis Pasteur, flipping pages and thinking I had to get out of there, somehow.

The bell rang and I walked right out the door, passing Miss Campbell on her way in to pick up our class. "John? Where are you going? John?" But I was running for the field, relieved by the cool air on my face, heading for the big oak, racing for cover.

A few minutes later Sandy found me behind the tree, and I learned what had happened.

"Sweat," she said, handing me the St. Christopher on the chain. "You wrote you think she is sweat. Here."

I took the medal, studying the saint standing mid-river with his staff, protectively carrying the small child on his shoulder.

"She says it's over," Sandy said. "Sorry," she added.

"It's okay," I said, pretending that I really meant it. I put the medal in my pocket. Above us a scrub jay screeched. Far away there were kids shouting, and a whistle blew. "When the bell rings will you walk in with me?"

"Sure," she said.

We stepped out into the field together.

◇ ABOUT THE AUTHOR

John Triska teaches third grade at Pacific Union School in Arcata, California. He has taught eighth grade and high school in the past. His students keep nature journals and travel to the Arcata Marsh weekly to follow seasonal changes in vegetation and bird life there. John has two daughters and lives in Arcata. He has been a teacher consultant with the Redwood Writing Project for ten years.

◇ NOTES FROM THE AUTHOR

This story is very simple. A sixth-grade boy misspells "sweet" as "sweat" and loses his chance at going steady with the girl of his dreams. I think what makes the story work is the element of surprise. The reader discovers the boy's mistake at the same moment the boy discovers it, when his next-door neighbor hands him back the medallion.

I owe the success of this story to my response group. I wrote the first draft of "Sweet" in three hours. So much of it was about me and my memories of elementary school; it just poured out of me onto the page. But when I read it aloud to my group, they said they already knew what was going to happen halfway through the story. In writing too much about the narrator's problems with spelling at school, I had given away the ending. They helped me see the place in the story where it was suddenly obvious the narrator was going to misspell the word. I wrote notes in the columns of my first draft and put it away for a few days.

After hours of rereading and revising, I decided to reveal the narrator's trouble with spelling by showing more about Mrs. Campbell. Then I added dates to the story, so it could start on Thursday and end on Friday, the day of Mrs. Campbell's spelling tests. I hoped readers would be fooled into thinking there was a spelling test coming up in the story, and wonder what that had to do with Gina. (Of course, the real spelling test, the one on the love note, had everything to do with Gina.) It did the trick. When I read my piece to a fresh audience, they got the foreshadowing that was needed to make the surprise ending work, but not enough to give it away ahead of time.

◇ WRITING CHALLENGE: USE FORESHADOWING

Experiment with foreshadowing in your writing. Look at a piece you have already written and see if you can insert some detail that will create a hint of what might be ahead. Let's say a character stumbles and drops a quarter, a dime, and her keys. She looks around and finds her keys and the quarter, but not the dime. It's just a dime, and she's in a hurry, so she gets in her car and begins driving. Later in the story her license plate number is announced on the radio as the winner of a thousand-dollar prize. She has 90 seconds to call the station and win. She pulls up to a phone booth and fumbles around in her pockets and purse for some change, but can only find the one quarter. She reads the notice on the phone, "Local calls, 35 cents." The reader thinks, "Oh, that's why she couldn't find the dime." When you read about the lost dime earlier, you may have wondered if that dime was going to be important, but you wouldn't have thought, "She'll need that dime later to win a thousand-dollar prize on the radio." Remember, it's just a shadow of something to come.

In your story you might intentionally misguide your reader into making a false conclusion so that your ending is a surprise. See what your response group thinks. By trial and error, you can learn to use foreshadowing to make your writing more powerful and convincing; just don't give away too much too soon.

BEES AND BAND-AIDS

◇◇◇◇◇◇◇◇◇◇◇◇◇◇◇◇◇◇

My favorite dress in second grade was a light cotton, blue flower print with a full skirt that would twirl around nicely without going up too high if I were in a twirly mood, and full sleeves loosely gathered at the elbow with elastic. Like most of my dresses, this one buttoned down the back. My mother had made it, and although she was an accomplished seamstress, she hadn't gotten the neck quite right, so it gaped open slightly. And somehow, on a bright, windy April day, on the playground during lunch recess, a bee managed to fly down my dress and get caught in my sleeve.

I was generally a calm child who prided herself on being controlled. If that sounds as if I was exceptionally mature, I wasn't—just self-conscious and somewhat aloof. During recess I had been eyeing the bees. They tended to cluster near the swings where dandelion, clover, and other flowering weeds covered the ground. I was very careful not to step on or otherwise antagonize them, but I also didn't totally avoid them, preferring to tell myself that they didn't really scare me. Otherwise, they would smell my fear and come after me in swarms.

So I dallied at the swings, waiting my turn, demurely twirling once in a while to feel the dance of cotton around my legs, when suddenly I felt a buzzing against my undershirt. I froze mid-twirl and stood very still, trying to will the bee not to exist. But the buzzing continued as the poor creature, who must by now have discovered it had not found its way into a giant exotic flower, began to buzz even louder as it made its way from my bodice to my sleeve.

After ten long seconds I threw all caution and self-control to the wind and began to scream and cry and flail at myself, trying simultaneously to both kill the bee and set it free. Help came running in the form of minions of other second graders who began to scream with me when they discovered I had been attacked by a bee. "Bees!" they screamed. "Bees!" I could hardly point out that it was only the one bee since it felt like a dozen. Our shrill chorus seemed to go on forever, but it could only have been a minute before I caught sight of my teacher, Mrs. Barnes, lumbering toward me.

Mrs. Barnes, with her graying red curls that bounced off the frames of her glasses when she moved quickly, as she was doing now, whose feet filled her solid shoes and overflowed, just a little at the ankle, whose hands had wrinkles and big brown spots on them like freckles, only different, was as divine to me now as the brightest angel I could imagine. I was engulfed as she pressed me to her ample bosom. Then shielding me with her large body, she nimbly unbuttoned my dress, whipped it over my head, shook it out, and had it back on me and rebuttoned before I had time to stop crying.

My screams stopped immediately; I was so shocked at this public undressing. But no one else seemed to have noticed, so I clung to Mrs. Barnes, weeping quietly in what I hoped was a ladylike fashion while she escorted me to the nurse, Mrs. West. They examined me and found that I had indeed been stung on the upper arm. Amazingly, I hadn't felt anything, but the terror of the bee itself had been so great that a mere bee sting was probably anti-climactic. I quieted in Mrs. West's office, and Mrs. Barnes hurried off to class as the bell rang. Sipping water, I pressed a cold washcloth to my face while Mrs. West put alcohol on the bee sting.

And then Mrs. West said, "Would you like a

 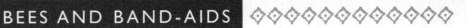

Band-Aid?" They were the words I didn't even know I had been waiting for, but when she said them I had to fight the urge to grab the Band-Aid box and spill its contents, as I searched for the perfect shape and size. "Yes, please," I said, using my most polite and grown-up voice. And even though I had not felt the sting and the minute bleeding had stopped and the little itch that was left after the stinger had been removed was a fading memory, I breathed a sigh of relief as the adhesive bandage was placed on my arm. Even though I knew that when I removed it later it would painfully tear the tiny hairs of my arm, I felt healed.

I lost my fear of bees after several years, although I never was one to seek them out. I thought I had also lost my love for Band-Aids until a few months ago when I found myself sitting in a small room with a different nurse, waiting for a vaccination. A needle was involved, and that needle engendered some of the same feelings the bee had 35 years ago. I didn't cry or cause a scene, even though I wanted to, but I fretted a little as the nurse rubbed alcohol on my arm just before piercing my flesh.

Surprisingly, I barely felt the shot; in fact, I complimented the nurse afterward on her gentle technique. She smiled, pleased at this, and dabbed my arm with a cotton ball. "I think you're bleeding a bit," she said. "Would you like a Band-Aid?"

"A Band-Aid?" I hesitated. Maybe I was too old for Band-Aids. But as I peered over my glasses, I could see a tiny spot of blood that seemed to reappear as fast as the nurse could wipe it away. "Yes, please," I said. "I'd like a Band-Aid."

As I felt the adhesive stick to my skin, the trauma subsided. Something was holding me together; I had been patched up. Suddenly, I understood that the healing power of a Band-Aid is not limited to children. For all of us, it is a symbol of the knowledge that we will not break apart, that whatever happened is now over, that help has arrived. It is a badge that tells the world you are a survivor.

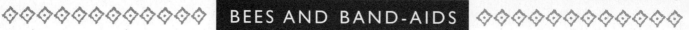

◇ ABOUT THE AUTHOR

Carol Billings has been a teacher consultant with the Redwood Writing Project since 1987. She has been teaching adult school in Eureka, California, for several years, but recently fell in love and moved to Oregon. That'll happen.

◇ NOTES FROM THE AUTHOR

When I write, all kinds of connections occur to me, and this time was no different. My memory of that bee sting reminded me of a psychology class in which I learned that the number one fear of second graders is bees. So, when I first shared this piece with my writing group, it began differently, with me as an adult in psychology class. That scene then led into the story of the bee sting. My writing group pointed out that the part about the psychology class was not relevant, and that it diluted the power of the story of the bee sting. I didn't agree with them at first, mostly because I became very attached to the words I put on the page, and I thought that part of the essay was particularly clever and well written. When I took it out, however, and concentrated on developing the bee sting story, I could see that my writing group was correct.

◇ WRITING CHALLENGE: USE SIGNIFICANT OBJECTS

Writers often use objects such as clothing to evoke memories of time, place, mood, characters, emotions, and events. Even after almost 45 years, Carol Billings can still see, feel, and even smell that dress. It wasn't just a piece of clothing, it was a beloved object that she connected to a particular time and place as if it were a witness to that part of her life. In this case, it was intimately involved with what happened because it possibly attracted the bee and definitely helped trap it. Think about a piece of clothing or other object that was intimately involved in an event in your life. Write about the event and let the object be a part of the story, not just part of the description of you.

Read "New Shoes" in this collection for another example of a story in which clothing plays a major part.

A NEW UNDERSTANDING

On Saturdays I sometimes walked to Jerry's, our neighborhood bookstore, and just looked around. Once I read silently a message on a yellowed piece of paper taped to the wall behind the cash register, "It's easy to learn the difference between right and wrong. What's hard is to tell the real from the imagined."

What does that mean? I thought. Now that I'd turned thirteen, subjects that I wouldn't have paid attention to three or four years earlier had become interesting.

I knew the difference between right and wrong. A crack team of experts had been working on my education in that field for my entire life. My Sunday school teachers, backed by Ten Commandments, provided weekly demonstrations of good and evil on the first day of each week. Mondays through Fridays for seven years a teacher at Raymond Avenue and then Osage Avenue school corrected my behavior and attitudes. Now, in junior high, I had six different teachers reinforcing my education with a constant barrage of "turn around" and "stop talking" and "get to work."

To top it off, my dad was a cop. He not only let me know each time I strayed from the path of righteousness, but in his vigilance to teach, he would detect and then point out every breech of legal or social convention around us. "Look at that guy changing lanes without signaling," he'd announce to the entire family while driving. He'd come back to the table at Woody's Smorgasburger on our family's semiannual night out to dinner and say, "That guy in the restroom didn't even wash his hands after using the toilet. What kind of parents did he have?" The sign in the bookstore was accurate—learning right from wrong was a piece of cake.

At that time in my life, I knew quite a bit about reality, too. I knew the most important activity in the world was to drive. Thus, sixteen, the age at which I would be able to legally drive, was the most important age. Driving a cool car was pretty important, too. I was getting a Corvette. T-birds were turning into luxury cars, and Mustangs and Camaros lived only in the minds of car designers. I'd already saved more money toward my Corvette than I'd ever accumulated at one time—three dollars.

Another thing I knew was that we kids were constantly observed by a huge adult communication network, ready to report our mistakes to our parents practically before we made them. Try to look cool smoking on the corner with your friends, and some adult will tell another adult who tells your parents before you even get home, and the first thing they do when you walk in the door is come up to you and take a big whiff of your clothes. Get in a rock fight in the bean field, come home with a little cut on your cheek, and your mom will say, "That cut doesn't look as bad as the one Billy Boyd got in the rock fight." Billy Boyd's mom has already called John Kaplan's mom who called Jimmy Patrick's dad who called your dad who told your mom. Almost before the last rock fell to earth, the whole neighborhood was grounded. If one adult knows something about you, every adult in the world instantly has that knowledge. I knew this to be true—until one weekend soon after my thirteenth birthday.

"We're leaving in fifteen minutes, are your clothes packed and in the car?" Mom asked.

"I don't want to go. I want to stay home," I whined. Trying to salvage my chances for a weekend alone I promised, "I'll take care of the animals while you're gone."

"We've been through this. You're going. You've never met your second cousins. You're too young to stay home alone. Besides, it's only for one night. We'll be back tomorrow for Sunday dinner."

Begrudgingly, I put spare clothes into my canvas duffel bag and joined the family in the station wagon. The drive to the Porters' went by quickly; my mom used the time to explain that Don was my dad's cousin, and their two boys, Steve and Mike, were our second cousins. Mike was my age, so a ray of hope began to shine on my mood; maybe I'd have fun on this trip after all.

As we pulled up to the big farmhouse, even I could see that Cousin Don had done well as a farmer. Their house was surrounded by hundreds of acres of cotton and sugar beets. I'd never been to a house where you couldn't even see the next-door neighbor. I was used to smelling what the McDougals were having for dinner and hearing Jimmy Franz get chewed out by his dad for neglecting to feed the dog "for the umpteenth time." We had closer neighbors than this on camping trips.

After our initial greetings, a quick tour of the house, and a big farm lunch, Don picked up his napkin with his leathery hands, wiped his mouth, and said, "Let's go for a ride in the airplane." I thought he was kidding; I never knew anyone who actually owned an airplane.

A large red barn stood across the road from the house. On the far side of that barn, under a shed roof, sat the Porters' airplane, a four-seat Cessna. This trip may work out great, I thought, as Dad, Don, Mike, and I soared over the southern San Joaquin Valley. I felt butterflies in my stomach. My pulse pounded at my temples. I had no idea that the next day would prove even more exciting.

Sunday morning breakfast featured scrambled eggs, bacon, ham, and piles of flapjacks. After breakfast Mike and I played a couple games of Yatzee, checked out his baseball cards, and played wiffle ball in the yard for an hour. During a lull in the action, Mike said, "Let's drive out to the pond."

"Just us?" I asked incredulously, knowing Mike was thirteen, too.

"Sure, I drive all the time," he replied nonchalantly, seemingly unaware of the incredible power and prestige he carried with that statement.

"Yeah," I said, "Let's go."

"Be back soon," Don ordered, handing Mike the keys, "Bob and his family are leaving for home in an hour."

Mike and I climbed into the Scout and headed out among the sugar beets and cotton. All the roads we traveled were on their farm, so we weren't breaking any laws, but I was thrilled by the freedom I felt —just the two of us, flying down the dirt roads.

"Wanna drive?" asked Mike.

"Sure," I replied. After all, I thought, there's no traffic and nobody to see us; what could go wrong? I'd already had some driving experience. I was good on bumper cars, and already knew that in real driving you didn't stop by smashing into another car or some solid object. And I'd been to Disneyland. I knew Mr. Toad's Wild Ride didn't count; you could spin and spin the steering wheel without affecting the direction of the car. It was on a track. But the Autobahn ride was different. The cars could actually be steered. You had about a foot on each side of the car before you ran into a curb, and I could travel the whole track without hitting either side. All I needed to do was add the brake concept to the mix, and I was ready for the Daytona Speedway.

I walked around the Scout and jumped in behind the wheel. Mike described the theory of the clutch, and after a couple of jackrabbit starts and stalls, I was off and running. I had it up to about 30 when Mike said, "Turn here," and pointed to a road to the left between two cotton fields. I released the gas pedal and swung the steering wheel hard to the left. The car began to drift slightly sideways. I panicked, cranked the wheel even more to the left, and slammed on the brakes. The wheels locked up. As the car began to spin, cotton fields and dirt roads whirled alternately beyond the windshield. The car bounced as we left the slick dirt road and entered the corner of a cotton field. We stopped, but could see nothing through the dust cloud that surrounded us.

"Are you okay?" Mike asked.

Am I okay? I thought. He probably wants to be sure I'm still alive so he can kill me with his bare hands. I was too petrified to answer him.

"Well, let's get out and check the car," Mike suggested. The news was not good. Though we had not done any crushing body damage, the car was high-centered on a mound of hard dirt in the corner of the field. Both front wheels were off the ground. Water spit straight down from the broken radiator, eroding a rapidly growing puddle filled with water I knew should remain in the engine if we were to progress from that point.

We stepped back to assess the situation. Actually, Mike was assessing the situation. I was counting the minutes I had left to live. At least when I was dead, I wouldn't have to continue feeling like the most stupid person ever born, or live with the guilt knowing that my carelessness had caused my cousin Mike to be grounded for the rest of his life.

Impotently, we heaved on the front bumper of the car, trying to push it off the mound on which it was suspended. We soon learned that we had a problem beyond the scope of our unassisted abilities. A pickup truck came bouncing up the road from the direction of the house. Cousin Don swung out of the truck, looked at the Scout, looked at us, and far more calmly than I would have expected, asked, "What happened?"

"It's my fault," I stammered. "I was driving, and I went off the road. It's my fault. I did it." If I had

learned one thing from all my right-from-wrong training, it was to admit to my mistakes, the sooner, and the more forcefully, the better. "I'm really sorry. I shouldn't have done this," I continued. Cousin Don by now was examining the underside of the Scout, and forming a plan.

"We need to get Bob back to the house," he said to Mike. "His parents are all packed up and ready to go. Anyway, we need a tow chain from the barn. Let's go." The three of us climbed into the cab of the pickup.

On the way back I apologized another 20 times, and after a brief silence, as more an obituary than a conversation starter, said, "My dad's going to kill me."

Don thought for a second, and replied, "He doesn't have to know."

The idea was so foreign to my belief in the ways of adults that the full impact didn't even register. "Of course he does. I have to pay for the new radiator. I mean he will, and I'll have to pay him back."

"Heck, we make repairs like this all the time," Don replied. "We had to completely rebuild a 70-horse diesel tractor last month. Now that's expensive. But it's the cost of doing business. A little radiator repair is nothing."

"But, we… I… um…" my voice trailed off as we approached the house.

"It'll be our little secret," he said to me with a quick wink, hopping out of the truck. "I found 'em out near the pond," Don announced to the group now waiting by our family station wagon. "The Scout overheated."

I piled into the car with my family and waved goodbye to the Porters. I glanced out the back window as we pulled onto the road and saw Cousin Don walking toward the barn to get a tow chain. I think he was whistling.

◇ ABOUT THE AUTHOR

Bob Sizoo has taught sixth grade in Eureka, California, since 1986. He is currently on leave from his teaching position to codirect the Redwood Writing Project. He has been a teacher consultant with that National Writing Project site since 1987. He lives in Fieldbrook, California, with his wife, three horses, and two cats.

◇ NOTES FROM THE AUTHOR

I wanted to show how my dad's cousin changed my view of adults, but I couldn't decide if it was about what a great guy he was or about what a dope I was. I decided it's about me, because I think the event was more pivotal in my life than it was in his.

The reader didn't learn much about Cousin Don until the big incident. You knew he was a successful farmer, but that's about it. Since it was an autobiographical incident about an important moment in my life, I didn't have to build his character. Had this piece taken the form of a biographical sketch, I would have needed to put more information about his life and circumstances. It's really both, and shows how difficult it can be to categorize writing by genre.

I wanted the story to end ambiguously, with a silent ride home. I considered adding a paragraph about the next time I saw cousin Don. It was 15 years later after my mom's funeral. We had a little reception with cake and punch at our house after the service. He walked by me and asked quietly, "Remember our little secret?" "Of course," I answered. Then other people mingled closer and the conversation ended. That was it. Do you think I should have kept that in the story?

◇ WRITING CHALLENGE: WRITE ABOUT SOMEONE YOU KNOW

Choose an autobiographical incident from your portfolio or write a new one. Find a strong character other than yourself and change the focus. Keep the point of view the same, that is, tell it in first person, but concentrate on exposing and describing the character. Think of it like this:

1. In an autobiographical incident, the focus on one particular moment in your life will include one or more other characters to help describe and define that moment.

2. In a firsthand biographical sketch, the focus is on one particular character in your life. You may include one or more moments to describe and define that character.

◇ BY KARIN COOK

BEAUTY

◇◇◇◇◇◇◇◇◇◇◇◇◇◇◇◇◇◇

I hadn't had a haircut with a name since my Dorothy Hamill. And there I was, the night before my sixth-grade graduation, about to get an "artichoke." My sister, Elizabeth, and I had gotten the idea to go short from a news story about a group of guys in the Midwest who shaved their heads in a show of support for a teammate with leukemia. Given notice, Mama would never have allowed that kind of cut; she planned to keep her hair as long as she possibly could. Mama liked hers best when it was twisted up the back. If she'd used more bobby pins, it could have been a lobster tail. Our pinkies linked in a promise, the way we'd have them when we were little; we made a pact to each cut the other's hair after dinner. We voted over a selection of photos and diagrams from *Seventeen* and *Young Miss* and settled on the artichoke because the top could be styled to either spike or curl. The caption under the drawing said, "For soft days and hard nights…the artichoke is the most versatile style around." I agreed to go first.

Elizabeth propped the diagram up on an empty chair and set out her tools. With her eyes narrowed in concentration, she combed my wet hair over my face, down past my chin, and cut around the top of my head, just above the eyebrows. Slick brown pieces fell onto my legs and covered the floor around me like twigs. She hummed as she worked to the tune of "Piano Man." Before long my hair was falling away from me in loose hunks. I could feel Elizabeth making mistakes, the sound of scissors clanking fiercely, the blades cold against my head. It didn't look anything like the artichoke I'd had for dinner at the Shaptaws' house the previous week. Not even upside down. Not even when I fluffed my hair with my fingers to make the top pieces stand up straight.

Afterward, she bent to the floor. "You want it?" she asked, gathering the longest pieces at one end and holding them out to me. "You could save it and make a braid."

I knew Elizabeth would back out even before she started to justify herself. It had gotten late, the scissors were wet and beginning to jam. I locked myself in the bathroom and refused to come out. I wet down my cowlick and singed my bangs with a curling iron, trying to get them to feather. In the mirror my head looked small, my eyes huge and hollow. Nothing like this had ever happened to Elizabeth.

After awhile, Mama knocked on the door. "Tilden, honey, come on out," she said. "Let's have a look."

"Never," I said.

"What about graduation?" Mama asked.

"I'm not going." I dunked my head under the running water and started over with the blow dryer.

"How short is it?" I heard Mama ask Elizabeth.

"Promise you won't be mad," she said.

"I won't."

"Promise."

"I promise," Mama said.

"It's pretty short," Elizabeth said, "like a boy's."

"Tilden, what would make you feel better?" Mama asked.

I told her that the only thing that would make me open the door was if she forced Elizabeth to get an artichoke, too.

"Will you come out if I get one?" Mama asked.

When I unlocked the door, Mama was waiting in the hall. "It looks pretty," she said, reaching out to comb what was left of my bangs over to one side with her fingernails. She sat me down on the lid of

the toilet and moved my hair back and forth under her hands. She pulled at some pieces near my neck. "We'll just get Lainey to clean up these edges."

Then she called Elizabeth into the bathroom. "I want to tell you girls something," Mama said, positioning herself between us and sitting on the edge of the tub. Elizabeth sat as far away as possible, on the counter near the sink, and kicked her heels against the cabinets.

"You're perfect the way you are," Mama continued, "don't ever change anything."

Mama said that focusing on beauty would distract us from what really mattered. It had always been her belief that beauty came in cycles. And that all women were beautiful in one of three ways: striking, classic, and inner. She said that to be strikingly beautiful meant that people would stop you on the street, do things for you that they might not otherwise do. "It is a beauty that elicits unusual responses," she said. "On the surface striking might seem like that best kind of beauty, but really, it prevents understanding."

Elizabeth gnawed at a hangnail, pulling it with her teeth until it bled.

"Don't you wish for striking beauty," Mama said, when she caught me staring at Elizabeth's blond mane. She looked me right in the eye. "It will prevent people from seeing you."

Classic beauty, on the other hand, was useful in that it told a great deal about a woman's life. It meant that her lineage was reflected in her face, and that over time, after she'd worn it through experience, it became her own. I remembered that Grandma had said that. Mama had come from a long line of classic beauties. Women who received their rewards later in life.

Elizabeth gazed at herself in the mirror, then over to me, looking for the resemblance. At twelve, she had already developed a reputation as a beauty. The junior high guys acted surprised each time she passed, as if the wind had been knocked out of them. Her blue eyes were set in close to her nose, and when she smiled, her full cotton-candy pink lips stretched to

expose one tilted front tooth. When we pressed our cheeks together, we shared Mama's face. Apart, left to my own face, I felt separate, more a glint of Mama than actually a part of her. I remembered overhearing Grandma say that Elizabeth had our father's features. I stared at her, trying to tease out the parts that were different from mine, looking for clues about him. Imagining him, all light and laughter.

Mama took her hair down from the twist at the back of her head and bent it up to see what an artichoke might look like on her. She smiled at her reflection and then said to me, "I'm going to ask Lainey to cut my hair, too. That way we'll both have new looks when you start up at the junior high."

Elizabeth looked impatient. "Can I go now?" she asked, her fingers drumming at her sides.

"Sure," Mama said, dismissing her. Then she turned to me and squeezed my arm. "Tilden, it isn't about hair, you know. The only beauty to strive for is inner beauty," she said. "That's what matters over the long haul."

Lainey came by at the end of her shift at the hair salon. It was nine o'clock, almost past our bedtime, and Elizabeth and I sat silently watching as Lainey quartered Mama's ponytail with rubber bands and began sawing the hair just above the top band with the scissors. Little pieces sprang free. Mama pulled and measured each strand against her chin. I watched her face for disappointment. But she smiled the way she always did in the world, making it hard to know what she thought. At the end, Lainey was left holding a solid rope of Mama's hair, like a tail. She dropped it in a plastic bag and set it aside. She glanced at the photo of the artichoke in the magazine and went on to give Mama some layers, talking through each step. When she held up the mirror, Mama dipped her chin to each side.

"You have a wonderful line," Lainey said. "You could even go shorter."

Mama blew her hair out with the dryer, fuller at the top and longer at her neck.

"She looks like Mrs. Brady from TV," Elizabeth

whispered to me.

"No, she doesn't," I said. "It's shorter." To me, she looked the way the model in the magazine had looked, just the way I wanted my hair to look—perfect layers with a wave in the back. Nothing ever came out right on me.

Lainey trimmed the jagged edges of my hair and painted my fingernails while Elizabeth sulked in the corner. It was almost eleven o'clock when Lainey left and Nick, our stepdad, came upstairs to investigate. He appeared apologetic as if he was intruding. I watched his expression, waiting to find surprise in his face. Instead, he smiled big at Mama and kissed her hard on the neck.

"I feel like I'm living with two Twiggys," he said over her shoulder.

I gave him a blank stare.

"That's a compliment," he said.

As we were cleaning up, sweeping stray hair into a prickly pile, Elizabeth picked Mama's rope of hair out of the bag and held it up to her nose, inhaling the smell of it deeply.

"Put that back," Mama said. Her tone was a shock: harsh and punishing; it made Elizabeth cry. Mama moved to comfort her. "I just don't want it floating around," she added softly.

The next morning I overslept, and by the time I arrived at Brooklawn Elementary, the entire sixth grade was lined up in the hall, ready to march. My friend Samantha leaned out of her place in line, showing off her sandals with wedge heels. Her hair was braided down her back with sprigs of baby's breath at the top and bottom.

"You look so different," she called to me.

The graduation march came over the loudspeaker in the gym, and just as we had rehearsed, the whole line swayed forward to the beat. As we walked slowly across the waxed gym floor, I looked at the bleachers to see if I could find Mama, but only the top of her head was visible over the crowd. The slow, hollow music made my throat tighten. When Mr. McKinney called my name, I felt hot

and flushed. Ms. Zimmerman squeezed my hand for a long time before giving me my scrolled certificate. Her touch almost made me cry.

That afternoon Elizabeth and I made up, silently, while Mama and Nick were out getting a cake. Mama's room was still, the light painting windowpanes on the carpet. I found Elizabeth up to her elbows in the large mahogany dresser by the bed. We moved wordlessly through Mama's things—holding up scarves, leg warmers, wooden beads—and draping each other in her favorites. At her closet we pushed through the hangers, coming by her fancy clothes: a denim dress, maroon skirt, and beige Angora sweater. These were the clothes Mama wore when she had something official to do involving the school or for any occasion when pictures might be taken. We slid pieces of these clothes on over our own and moved around the room like grown women.

It was Elizabeth who found the wig, the one Mama would need after her hair fell out from the chemotherapy, hidden at the back of the closet, tucked away behind Mama's shoe boxes and shrouded in tissue paper. She put her hand out as if to touch a shy dog and brought the wig into the light. Neither of us said a word. Round, with stiff dirty blond hair similar to my own, the wig looked more like an overgrown cabbage than an artichoke. Elizabeth folded her thick blond hair up and tucked in the stray pieces with her free hand. From an angle, in the mirror, she looked almost exactly like me. For a moment, I was filled with pride. Myself, but better. It wasn't the right feeling, I knew. Looking at her, I imagined for the first time what it would really feel like to be beautiful. Elizabeth turned from side to side in front of the mirror, making pouty, sexy faces, watching herself from all angles.

No matter what Elizabeth did, I would always look more like Mama.

From *What Girls Learn* by Karin Cook. Reprinted by permission of International Creative Management, Inc. Copyright © 1999 Pantheon.

◇ ABOUT THE AUTHOR

Karin Cook is the author of the novel, *What Girls Learn*, from which this story is taken. She runs a corporate mentoring program at an advertising agency and works with youth at The Door, a multi-service youth center in New York City. She is working on a new novel, *Sweat*, about horses, contagion and quarantine. She splits her time between New York and Provincetown, Massachusetts.

◇ NOTES FROM THE AUTHOR

I write from a place of feeling haunted by small moments and memories—a bit of conversation, an object of great power, a knowing glance between people. It seems to me that memory is made up of emotionally loaded moments that can be captured with careful attention to detail. In this chapter of my novel, I utilized many of the details that haunted me from my experience of my own mother's struggle with breast cancer in order to make these characters' emotional experience ring true.

I was careful to juxtapose the narrator, Tilden's, concern with her own physical appearance with her worries over her mother's changing appearance because of the effects of her illness and treatment. I wanted to raise questions about the importance of appearance in our culture and to broaden the definition of beauty to go beyond looks, hair, and clothes to include the essence of who we each are—a crucial lesson that Mama passes onto her daughters during her battle with breast cancer.

How do sensory details (a brightly colored item of clothing, a particular smell, the way something feels to the touch) inform memory? Why is this kind of detail so important in storytelling?

◇ WRITING CHALLENGE: USE SYMBOLISM

Hair plays an important part in our culture. If our hair's dark, we dye it blond. If it's gray, we dye it dark. If we have straight hair, we get it curled. If it's too curly, we straighten it. If there's too much, we shave it off, pluck it, or cover it with wax and rip it out. If there's not enough, we put chemicals on our heads to make it grow. We're nuts about our hair. When I was in junior high, Billy Watson's grandpa told him that if he rubbed chicken manure on his upper lip, his mustache would grow in faster. I don't think he tried it, but then again, he didn't have chickens.

Eyes may be a window to the soul, as Shakespeare said, but historically, hair has played many roles in literature, as well. Samson lost his strength when his hair was cut, and some religious groups insist that women wear their hair long because in I Corinthians it says if a woman has long hair, "…it is a glory to her." In *House on Mango Street,* Sandra Cisneros describes her mother's hair as "sweet to put your nose into…when she is holding you, holding you and you feel safe… the warm smell of bread before you bake it."

In "Beauty," Karin Cook has written a story in which hair means far more than just decoration or style. It represents a powerful bond between a girl and her dying mother, and thus, in literary terms, it is a symbol. Make a list of all the stories in your life in which hair plays a part. Choose one from the list to write about, showing hair as something more than just the fur that grows on your body. Or choose another attribute or object and use it as a symbol.

THE PARTY

It didn't take me long to figure out that I wasn't invited to the party. I got off the bus and saw my friends huddled under the tree where we all stood every morning before the first bell. There were six of us: Theresa, Becky, Barbara, Carol, Kim, and me. I can't even say that we were close friends. We had come from different elementary schools and never fit with the predictable middle school jocks, pops, or nerds. We were flotsam and jetsam that washed under a tree in front of the library and became an entity by default and by simply standing together.

The circle seemed tighter as I approached; the flittering of small white envelopes being hastily stuffed into backpacks and binders gave it away. I knew as well as the entire universe that Bridget's party was this weekend. Bridget was one of the pops, the popular ones and the antithesis of me. She was thin and wore clothes that looked like they came straight from the pages of magazines. She had that hair—red, and cut into a perfect page, smoothed into a bowl around her face, and every shade of shoes to match even her wildest outfits. She had a select group of followers who squealed and hugged each other between every class, as if they hadn't seen each other in years. We all wanted to be like her or them and being invited to her party meant elevation in the school pecking order. To not be invited meant standing in stagnant water.

My stomach churned, and I hoped that Bridget was still holding an envelope with my name on it to be delivered later. But my friends' shuffling feet and furtive glances guaranteed my fate. Their too-eager hellos told me that everyone already knew who was invited and who wasn't.

"Hi," I responded, but that one word already sounded hollow with disappointment.

Becky, always the diffuser of uncomfortable moments, said, "Hey, did you get all the algebra homework done?"

"Everything but the last problem," I mumbled.

"Here, want to see the answer?" Eagerly, maybe out of guilt, she gratuitously flipped open her binder before I could tell her it didn't matter.

I pretended to be interested in her calculations but my head swam with that sinking feeling that there was something wrong with me. That I wasn't worthy.

Thankfully, the bell rang and I hurried toward English. When I passed the cafeteria, the impending lunch smells followed me, and I felt nauseous by the time I reached class, but I knew it wasn't from the aroma of creamed turkey and overcooked green beans. I couldn't concentrate on the short story we were supposed to be reading in class, but I had no trouble attending to the faux wood grain on my desk and wondering if I could dissolve into it and disappear.

Why hadn't she invited me? My feet were too big? No. Maybe. My face was broken out? Who wants someone with acne at her party? Why did she invite every person in my group except me? I tried to think of any interactions I'd had with Bridget recently. A few days earlier, we'd been partners during a sixth-period project. I was intent on getting the project done and impressing her with the grade we could get, and she was intent on looking at teen magazines. She barely spoke to me except to say, "You're so serious. You know, you should smile more."

By the end of second period, I had overheard all the details about the party. They were going bowling.

It was a sleepover. There was going to be a scavenger hunt. They were renting scary movies and were going to stay up all night. Each time someone mentioned the party, I smiled weakly and nodded.

During third period, Meredith, one of the drama club girls, who wasn't invited and didn't care, asked me if I was going to Bridget's party.

Instead of saying no, I found myself repeating tidbits that I'd heard earlier. "Her dad is taking everyone to IHOP for breakfast. They're taking two big vans so everyone will fit." I said it with authority. As if I were going, too.

Meredith said, "I wish she'd invited me so I could tell her no. She's such a brat. And all that phony hugging. What's that all about, anyway?"

Where did Meredith get her confidence? I wondered.

At lunch, I sat with my group at our usual table, and they politely avoided the subject. When Kim got up to take her tray, she said, "I'm going shopping tomorrow after school. Anybody want to come?"

But I knew what they would be shopping for, so I said, "I can't. I'm busy."

Becky hung behind and walked with me to dump our trays.

"I heard Bridget could only invite so many people."

"Whatever," I said. "See you later." I didn't look at Becky. I couldn't look at her because if I saw any pity or kindness in her eyes, I'd start crying so I pretended to look for something seemingly important in my backpack until she left.

Maybe she didn't invite me because of my hair. It's so long and stringy. Maybe it's my coat. It is pretty ugly compared to some of the other girls' coats. I should have bought another color. But what does it really matter? None of my clothes match. I'm way too tall but there isn't anything I can do about that, and she couldn't not invite someone to a party because they were too tall, could she? Maybe I should smile and hug more but I just can't get into

hugging people unless I know them really well. Probably if I'd smiled more, I would have been invited.

I hated Bridget. I hated her more for having the ability to make my life miserable. I wanted to go home. I felt sick. As I changed classes, I averted my eyes from everyone I knew so I wouldn't have to smile. So I wouldn't have to pretend that I was likeable.

By fifth period, the news was out. Three girls that had been invited to the party couldn't go because of the overnight band trip. They rushed up to Bridget to tell her the sad news, and one of them cried, proving what a good friend she was and how much she wanted to go. They gave back their invitations. I passed the crier between classes and saw her injured, yet superior look. After all, she had been invited.

Then the whispers began, like tiny wisps of drifting clouds, about who might be chosen in their places. I walked to sixth period, trailing behind Bridget, hanging back and watching hopeful faces laughing a little too loudly as they passed her. I counted nine girls who smiled and said hello to her on the short walk between classes. They might as well have been saying, "Choose me. Choose me."

After school, Becky found me in the bus lines. Breathlessly, she said, "Bridget asked Barbara at lunch who else she should invite, and Barbara said you. And Kim just told me that she just heard Bridget say she was going to *maybe* invite you to her party. Call me, okay?" She held up both hands with fingers crossed, then hurried toward her bus.

There was still a chance. But what did Becky mean when she'd said Bridget was *maybe* going to invite me. Was there a condition?

Over all the heads, I could see the red hair bobbing toward the bus lines, then stopping. I heard Bridget laughing. She moved to another group, and there was another little burst of laughter.

Kids began crunching forward to board the bus.

So what if I don't go to the party. I'm still me

whether I go or not. And it's just for one night. So what's the big deal? My thoughts were spinning. Bridget headed toward my line, weaving through the crowd, and it did seem as if she was headed toward me. I pretended to not notice and looked straight ahead at the bus.

I felt a hand on my arm.

I turned my head.

Bridget held out an invitation. "Will you come to my party?"

I looked at the small envelope, relishing the moment. But my mind was a jumble. Now she wanted me to come to her party, but she hadn't wanted me in the beginning. I am an afterthought. I am not on the A list. I'm just filling a space so the vans will be full. I need to smile more.

Take it, I thought. You know you want to go. Take it.

The crowd was moving me now, and I was only a few feet from the bus steps. Bridget moved with me as I inched forward, still offering the invitation. I looked at the envelope. The original name had been scribbled out but my name hadn't even been written in its place. If I didn't take it, I was sure that it would go to someone else.

I put my foot on the first step of the bus, then looked at her.

I hesitated.

Someone behind me yelled, "Get on the bus!"

I took a deep breath and gave her my answer.

And then, I smiled.

◇ ABOUT THE AUTHOR

Pam Muñoz Ryan grew up in Bakersfield, California. She was a bilingual teacher and an early child-hood administrator until she became a full-time writer in 1992. She has written over 20 books for young people, including the acclaimed *Amelia and Eleanor Go for a Ride* (An ALA Notable Book), *Riding Freedom,* and most recently, *Esperanza Rising.* She lives in north San Diego County with her husband and four children.

◇ NOTES FROM THE AUTHOR

One of my most vivid memories of junior high school is of not being invited to a popular girl's party and then, at the last minute, being invited because someone else couldn't go. I still remember how pervasive, dominating, and painful this experience was and how it made me question my worth and self-esteem. As adults we often trivialize incidents like this in a young adolescent's life, forgetting how their emotions can encumber many of their daily routines, interactions, and responsibilities.

I purposely didn't let the reader know the outcome. What do you think this character decided? What would the reader have done? Why?

◇ WRITING CHALLENGE: TRY AN AMBIGUOUS ENDING

I saw the movie *Cast Away* last night. The movie ends with Tom Hanks, the star, standing at a cross-roads in rural Texas. He has to make a decision of where to go next in his life, but the movie doesn't tell us what that decision is going to be. I read that the movie was also filmed with a more tradition-al "happy ending," but the director wanted to leave a little question in the minds of the audience. After the movie, we talked about what the character was going to do next.

Fairy tales have a more certain ending, and often end with the phrase, "They all lived happily ever after." Try reading a fairy tale and leave out the last few lines. Think about possible endings for the story other than the traditional ending.

Did you like the way "The Party" ended? Were you afraid that the author would cave in to her desire to be with the popular girls and go to the party after all? Did you want to hear all the details about how she refused Bridget's invitation, maybe even in the way Meredith might have? Pam Muñoz Ryan told this story well. We cared about the main character and really wanted her to do the right thing. But she cut the story off before we could find out her response to the invitation. An ending like this often gives you more to think about and talk about than one that ties a story up in a neat little package.

Can you think of other stories you've read or seen in a movie that ends ambiguously? Try an ambiguous ending on a story you are writing, or pick a story from your portfolio and revise it to leave the reader with a question at the end. Read it aloud to your class or response group or have a friend read it and find out what your audience thinks about your ambiguous ending.

For Maha

BEATING A BULLY

◇◇◇◇◇◇◇◇◇◇◇◇◇◇◇◇◇◇◇◇◇

I was in the eighth grade and my sister Maha was in the fifth when our family moved to a new town. It happened all of a sudden, and without much discussion. We had lost the only home we had owned shortly after the 1967 war in Palestine, and since then had to uproot many times in search for a town where Dad could work and we could rent a house. I don't know what Maha felt about the move, because she was a shy girl and hardly talked back about anything. But I did not like leaving all of my friends behind and made sure everyone knew that.

In the new school I tried hard to get along with the new crowd. I pretended to like everything the popular girls liked—the way they stretched their words as they spoke through chewing gum; the way they coiled their long hair behind their heads, like spare tires on the backs of army jeeps; the long gossip sessions they had about someone they all knew and I didn't; and the way their eyes sparked coyly as they spoke about movie stars. I also made myself laugh at the things they laughed at although inside I felt so lonely.

That quickly changed when I realized that there was nothing I could do to fit in with a group of girls that had spent many years together before my arrival. So I focused on studying, and in a short time, it became known that I would get the highest grades in all of my classes. Many girls then sought my friendship, and that made me feel stronger. But not when it came to a girl named Nahida.

On the first day Maha and I came to school, during recess, Nahida came to check us out. I was sharing a sandwich with Maha when Nahida snatched the food from my hand and began to eat it. When she was done, she threw the rest on the ground and left. Nahida was bigger than me and looked older. That made me scared to say anything. Maha, who often walked with her head down, now covered her face and began to cry. I pretended that nothing unusual had happened. When Nahida finally left us, a girl from my class came and whispered that Nahida was the strongest girl on the ground. She could beat up anyone she wanted, and no one would stop her. Nahida's dad was the principal at the boy's school, and our teachers did not want to upset him so they overlooked Nahida's actions, the girl explained.

Maha and I decided not to tell our mother about Nahida, because Mom had told us in the beginning of the year that if we got involved in any trouble, she would take us out of school without any discussion. Our teachers also had warned on the first day of enrollment that any fights would lead to dismissal of all those involved.

So after that day, during recess time, Maha and I would hide to eat our food, occasionally in the bathroom—in order to avoid Nahida's anticipated demand for a share. That made Nahida leave me alone, but she continued to go after my sister. She sought her out and hit her almost every day.

Girls would come and tell me that they had just seen Maha crying. I would run and ask Maha about what happened. But Maha would wipe off her tears and say that no one had hit her. She didn't want Nahida to hit me, too, if I got involved. That lasted for a long time, until I decided I could no longer tolerate my fear of Nahida or her beatings of Maha.

I could not sleep the night I made that decision. I kept on imagining myself fighting with Nahida. When I would reach the moment of making her cry, I would become too tense and would go to get a drink of water. My mother noticed I was not able to sleep and asked if I was all right. I said I was anxious about a test I was having the following day.

In the morning, and seemingly without a cause, I told my mother that if she ever took me out of school, I would use all of my grade A intelligence to make her and everyone in the family miserable. I didn't wait for an answer from her and rushed out to school. Maha followed me as if I were her mother and she a kitten of mine.

During the first two classes, I could not hear any of what my teachers said. I was only thinking of Nahida. At last, recess arrived. I chose to walk out with two girls whom I'd helped with homework often in the past. I told them I was going to search for my sister and would like to keep an eye on her from afar.

Maha stood on the playground with a group of her friends. Nahida ran up and hit her. She pushed a couple of girls aside and pulled Maha's braid to the ground. I ran to Maha. When Maha looked up and saw me, she started to sob loudly. That made me forget my fear. I found myself turning to Nahida, and I threw my entire body against hers. Nahida fell to the ground. I got up and slammed myself on her chest. Everything I had seen my brothers do during their fights with boys came into my mind.

I hit Nahida in the face, and I clenched my hands around her neck. I felt the rage I'd been holding back surge through me and strengthen my hands. I told her that I would kill her if she touched my sister again. I spit on her face. Then I asked Maha to come and hit Nahida before all was over. Despite her trembling, Maha arched down and pulled Nahida's hair.

The entire school had gathered around us by then, but no one attempted to do anything about the fight. When the teachers and the principal came, they asked that I immediately get off Nahida's chest. I screamed at the top of my lungs that Nahida had been hitting my sister every day for a long time.

When Nahida and I stood up, her hair looked like a thorn bush; her clothes were torn up, and her face was covered with tears. I heard giggles come from behind me and knew it must have been someone Nahida had hit before. But I did not feel a victory. I knew I was going to be dismissed from school, and that my mother would soon punish me for adding yet another conflict to her problem-filled days.

"Go home and come back with your mother," the principal said with a stern voice.

I had nothing to say and walked out of school. Maha wanted to come with me, but I asked her to go back to her class. One girl yelled out that she would take care of my books and bring my school bag home. Another girl said she would take notes from the classes I would miss.

I didn't go home. I sat under a tree for four hours and waited for Maha to walk by. We walked home together. Before we entered the house, Maha reached out and held my hand. She said thanks. That made both of us cry.

At home Mother could read our faces and knew that something terrible must have happened. When she asked, I told her I did not want to talk, and that I hated her with all my heart. Maha told the story.

Mother came with Maha and me to school the next morning. When all the students lined up before going into their classrooms, the principal asked that anyone who had been hit by me before that day raise their hands. No one did. She then asked those who were hit by Nahida to raise their hands. Several girls waved. The principal told everyone that from then on, if Nahida attacked them, even once, they would need to report it immediately. Nahida would then be expelled from school permanently.

Nahida and I were made to apologize to each other in front of everyone. When it was my turn to say sorry, I looked into her eyes and knew I was not sorry at all. I was happy that I was no longer scared. I looked at my mother, and to my surprise, she seemed to understand. Many girls wanted to be friends with me after that incident. That felt good. But what got printed on my mind was how Maha no longer walked with her head down. During recess she and I would pass each other by, and she would smile. The first time she did that, I could see the tender look in her eyes tell me she finally felt secure. That day, I felt strongest of all.

◇ ABOUT THE AUTHOR

Ibtisam S. Barakat lives in Columbia, Missouri. She leads Write Your Life workshops and creative writing workshops for high school students. Her writing addresses healing the hurts of racism, sexism, and the oppression of young people. She has been published by Collegiate Press, Perfection Learning, Simon and Schuster for Young Readers, Random House for Young Readers, and Pocket Books. For the past three years she has worked for the University of Missouri Extension Services, writing and programming for young people and child-care providers.

◇ NOTES FROM THE AUTHOR

I believe that everyone owns a gold mine of memories. And I think that a memory can be turned into a spectacular story like a piece of raw gold can be turned into earrings or a heart-shaped charm.

Before I wrote "Beating A Bully," my most vivid memory was of the moment I decided to hit Nahida in order to break the cage of fear I was in. I didn't recall all of the details, though, so I called my sister Maha and asked her about what she remembered. I also asked for her permission to use her real name. We laughed so hard each time Maha got to the part of pulling Nahida's hair. I also got input from a friend of mine because I didn't want the story in anyway to suggest that beating another person is all right. However, I wanted to show that a girl can be physically very powerful and can fight well even when feeling scared.

◇ WRITING CHALLENGE: WRITE ABOUT OVERCOMING AN OBSTACLE

In an earlier story in this collection, "How We Won the Bean Field War," the main character struggles to find a way to "beat the bully" by outsmarting him. The author of "Beating a Bully" didn't think she had that option. She felt better afterward, not because she hurt someone, but because she successfully overcame a huge obstacle. We know this because she "felt strongest of all" not when she beat another person, but when she saw her sister hold her head up, smiling. Make a list of obstacles you have overcome. It may have to do with friends or family, a physical hardship, or even your schoolwork. Choose one of these instances to write about. Try to show through dialogue or description yours and others' reaction to your success, instead of telling the reader something like, "I was really proud."

TICKLING A TROUT

◇◇◇◇◇◇◇◇◇◇◇◇◇◇◇◇◇◇

Potash isn't a big mountain. But the way it rises vertically, like a granite plug pushed up from the earth, makes it dramatically evident from the road as you drive from the town of Hadley toward Lake George. The view from the top makes the steep half hour scramble up its side more than worthwhile.

That summer day, as a locust in a nearby maple droned a whining song sharp enough to cut through stone, nine of us gathered at the base of the mountain to do just that. My wife and our two small sons, my sister Marge, my sister Mary Ann and her family started onto the trail by the cold water brook that flows along the mountain slope. But I stopped. My eyes had caught the flash of a square tail in the ripple just before it disappeared from sight. Whenever I glimpse a fish that way, I remember when Grampa Jesse showed me how to tickle a trout.

* * * * * * *

Though he didn't talk about it, Grampa Jesse was Abenaki Indian. He never said anything he taught me when I was a child had to do with that heritage. It was for me to figure out later in life when I would try to raise my own children the way he and Grama Bowman brought me up—never hitting me, giving me the freedom of the woods and the streams, showing me more by example than by telling me what to do and what not to do.

I was in sixth grade. Aside from getting high grades and being the first one with the answers, I wasn't doing that well. I was one of the smallest kids in my class. I had glasses. I was from the outlying countryside beyond the town of Saratoga Springs where I went to School Number 2—and thus, by definition, a "hick," far from being "cool," a new term just creeping into our vocabularies. I also read too many books, was not good at sports, and told my teacher whenever anyone picked on me. Thus, I was a brain, a nerd, and a squealer all in one neat package. I felt cursed.

When that summer came, fishing season came with it. It both excited and worried me. My dad, with whom I spent very little time, was a taxidermist and an outdoorsman of the first rank. When he went fishing, he always caught his limit; when he hunted, he always got his deer. Sooner or later, I knew, he would take me trout fishing. Sure enough, on a glorious day in late June, he did just that. As always, my sister Mary Ann went along. Dad brought three spinning rods to fish with. One was his own, one was Mary Ann's, and one was for me to use. At the lake Mary Ann was the first to cast her spinner into the water from the dock. After years of practice, she was an ace with a spinning rod. She caught a trout on her first cast. I tried throwing out my line, the unfamiliar rod as awkward as a club in my hand. The line whirred and tangled. A backlash. My father said something under his breath and grabbed the pole from me.

"I'll cast it for you. You can just reel it in. You can do that, can't you?"

I nodded. If I'd tried to say anything, I would have burst into tears.

When I got home late that afternoon, my father dropped us off in front of my grandparents' general store. I handed Grama a string of ten fat brook trout.

"You did so well, Sonny," she said.

"No, I didn't." I said. "I only caught one little

trout, and Dad said it was too small. Mary Ann caught all these." And then I started to cry. I buried my head against my grandmother's shoulder and sobbed. Why was it that I couldn't ever do anything right?

My grandfather's leathery hand was patting my shoulder, but he didn't say anything then or at dinner. He waited until the next morning.

"Come on," he said. We climbed into the old square blue Plymouth and drove up 9N, turned onto Porter Corners Road, and on up the mountain where he parked the car near the South Branch. Then and there, he showed me how to tickle a trout, how to coax it into your hands and lift it out of the water. It wasn't easy, and I was soon soaking wet, but I kept trying until I finally succeeded, until a seven inch brook trout was gently moving in my hands.

"What do I do now?" I said.

"Did you ask it to trust you?" Grampa asked.

I nodded. Grampa nodded back. I carefully lowered my hands and let the trout go.

It was an unusually hot, dry summer that year. By late August, Bell Brook, the little stream behind my grandparents' old house was going dry in places, leaving trout stranded in shrinking pools. I walked the creek with a bucket, rescuing trout to carry them further upstream where the water still flowed.

*   *   *   *   *   *   *

"There's a trout there," I said. Everyone looked, a little too late.

"No, there's not," said my sister Mary Ann. Only three words, but they invoked the old rivalry that had been set up in our childhood.

My two sons looked up at me. I didn't want to argue, but there had been a trout. I answered in as neutral a tone as I could. "There is," I said. "It's a brook trout, about a fourteen incher. It's under that flat rock there."

Mary Ann laughed. "There is not a fourteen inch trout there," she said. "You don't know that."

I sat down, took off my T-shirt, my shoes and socks. Then I waded in and walked slowly to that flat rock. Moving my hands with the flow of the current, a finger's width at a time, I slid my palms up under the stone, along the gravelly bottom until I felt the fanning movement of the trout's fins and then the silk smoothness of its belly. It wasn't just the slow movement of my hands that was important. Grampa Jesse had told me that. It was what I had in my mind, what I was thinking that counted. No hurry about it, no greed, no anger, just being calm. Asking the fish to trust you, asking it to give itself to you in a way that was as much a song as it was a wish. I slid my hands out from beneath the stone and lifted them from the water. The big hook-jawed male trout lay quietly in my hands, even though its bright pattern of spots, its glistening sides, were exposed to the air. I held it up so that everyone on the bank, some of them open-mouthed, could see.

"You're right," I said. "It's not a fourteen incher. More like eighteen." Then I lowered it into the stream, tipped my hands, and watched it laze back under the sheltering stone.

TICKLING A TROUT

◇ **ABOUT THE AUTHOR**

Joseph Bruchac has published several books including, *Hoop Snakes, Hide Behinds, and Side-hill Winders—Adirondack Tall Tales; Walking with My Sons; The Boy Who Lived With the Bears;* and the autobiographical, *Bowman's Store.*

◇ **NOTES FROM THE AUTHOR**

In the years that have passed since that day in June, I've caught many trout that way, always returning them to the water again. I've grown to be tall and strong, to be an athlete, to have friends, to raise children of my own. But that little boy who couldn't catch a fish with a pole is still there inside me. And he smiles as I am smiling now at the thought of how much began with that gift of trust my grandfather gave me when he taught me how to tickle a trout.

Writing, I always tell people, isn't that hard to do. But good writing, writing other people will want to read, is never easy. For me, the first draft of a story is only the first step on the journey. Even before this piece was sent to my editor, I rewrote it three times. In rewriting I cut out things that I realized might have been interesting to me but weren't really needed. My hard work paid off when the story was accepted for publication. However, my journey wasn't over yet. My editor sent the story back to me with some suggestions for revisions that felt, at first, as if I was being asked to cut off a few fingers. For one, he thought that the middle of the story should actually be the end. That was a hard road for me to follow. However, after a few days of reading and rereading his suggestions, I realized that he was right. A good editor (or a sensitive teacher) is like a guide who knows the best trails to take. As a result of listening to his advice, this story was much more successful in reaching its destination.

◇ **WRITING CHALLENGE: WRITE ABOUT SOMEONE WHO TEACHES BY EXAMPLE**

Joseph Bruchac's grandfather taught him by example instead of telling him what to do and what not to do. Think of someone close to you who teaches by example. Write about one such instance, or write about a time you have taught something to someone else by example. For instance, maybe you have shown someone how to be a good friend, instead of demanding that person be a good friend to you.

Also try this: A strong element in this story is the tension between Joseph Bruchac and his sister, a sibling rivalry. His sister was always a favorite of their father, adding to the feelings of inferiority that Joseph had to fight as a young boy. When he proves to his sister that he not only saw a large trout but could catch it in his bare hands, he appears to be trying to gain respect from her he rarely felt before. This theme is present in literature from the story of Cain and Abel in the book of Genesis in the Bible, to three sisters vying for their father's love in Shakespeare's *King Lear*, to two brothers fighting for their father's approval in John Steinbeck's *East of Eden*. Face it, siblings compete.

Write about a incident you experienced in which sibling rivalry plays an important part. This may be a rivalry between you and a sibling or someone else in the story and his or her sibling.

◇ BY SUSAN BENNETT

CROSSING THE LINE

◇◇◇◇◇◇◇◇◇◇◇◇◇◇◇◇◇◇

When I was twelve years old, I stayed with my grandparents, who were taking caring of me while my parents went on a vacation by themselves. My grandparents lived in Minnesota but I was born and reared in Ohio—a two days' drive away in those days, before six lane super highways. So, really, my grandparents and I were nearly strangers. Since I had been a small child, I had only spent brief time periods with them—a week here, two weeks there. And, my parents had always been around to help me understand their English since neither grandparent had been born in the United States. Now, I had a whole month to get used to their funny accents, strict rules, and "old-fashioned" expectations. They believed "children should be seen and not heard," and that twelve-year old girls were still too young to go off and do things by themselves.

For the first couple of weeks, I was content to follow their regulations. Three other girls my age lived on their block and since Hibbing was such a small town, everybody looked after each other and knew everybody's business. I was allowed to go to the movies with my new friends only because my grandmother knew the wife of the owner. And we could wander down Main Street all day and go to my grandfather's best friend's drug store and buy ice cream cones for a nickel. But their permissive attitude changed drastically the day I asked if I could go to the County Fair with Ann, and Laura, and Julie.

"That's no place for a nice girl to go without grown-ups," my grandmother cautioned.

"There's nasty people there," my grandfather roared. "Thieves and murderers, and kidnappers. Who grab little girls and they're never seen again! No granddaughter of mine will be caught dead in such a place. What would I tell your mother if you disappeared? Forget it!"

"But…but…but…" I stammered, shocked by my grandfather's outburst but still determined to go. "My parents let me go to the State Fair in Ohio with my friends right before I came here," I lied. "And I brought my babysitting money so it won't cost you anything. And I'll stay with Ann and Laura, and Julie. And, we'll be home before it gets too dark. I promise I won't do anything wrong and I won't talk to any strangers."

My grandparents looked at each other with resigned expressions. "Okay," my grandfather said. "But you better be home by dark."

"And don't say we didn't warn you," my grandmother added. "Be sure you put your money in a safe place and be careful of pickpockets."

"And stay away from them fortune-tellers and con men in the midway. They can see a sucker coming a mile away. A fool and his money are soon parted," shouted my grandfather.

"Sure," I agreed, although I had no idea what a midway or con man was, and I had never seen a fortune-teller in real life though I read about one in a book once, and my friend Ann had showed me her Ouija Board but we hadn't tried it yet. As I ran down the street to meet my friends before my grandparents had a chance to change their minds, I wondered what they meant about fools and money, but as soon as I spotted Ann, Laura, and Julie on the corner of Second and Main Streets impatiently waiting for me, I forgot all of my grandparents' admonitions and all of my promises except for the one about being home before dark.

Even after forty years, I can still taste that county fair hot dog slathered with mustard and the cloying, sweet, pink cotton candy. I can smell the pungent odor of the animals in the show arenas, and hear the cries of lost children and of frantic parents stripped of the last vestiges of patience. I can see the swirls of color as gaily dressed farm folks parade by, carousels spin, and Ferris wheels carry their passengers to heights of ecstasy, hysteria, and nausea. And I can feel that delicious combination of anticipation, excitement, and fear that only a twelve-year old alone with five dollars in her pocket at the County Fair can know.

Even for us kids "looking for adventure," the sordidness of the forbidden midway was almost more than our adolescent sensibilities could handle. Our struts became less certain, our voices subdued, our giggles less flirtatious. As we entered the world of missing teeth, cigarette-stained fingers, children aged by years on the road, missed school days, and squalid trailers, we grew timid and solemn. We recognized that the girl, pregnant and sweating, running the gold fish game was not much older than we; nor was the boy, tattered jeans and tattoo reading BORN TO LOSE, who ran the ring toss. None of us could admit to each other, let alone ourselves, that we could not distinguish our feelings of fascination from those of disgust, and yet on some level we envied them. By now—more part of the carnival than the lives we were there to escape—we, like Pinnochio, entered that forbidden world, the one we had all promised to avoid, the land of the "Carnies."

"Hey, Sweetie. How about giving the ball a roll?" called a barker in a conspiratorial tone. "Win yourself a teddy bear! Aw, come on. Don't be chicken. What can ya lose? Three balls for a lousy quarter! Tell ya what. Don't spread it around and I'll give ya a few practice rolls. Been a slow day. My boss'll never know the difference. Haven't given away so much as a whistle today. Somebody's bound to win now and then. You look like a nice girl. Couldn't be more 'an fifteen

now, could ya. What?! You're just twelve?! Coulda fooled me. Come on. Take a few free rolls. What'll it cost ya? Change your mind and you can just walk away. Nobody be the wiser. Here, lemme show ya."

I fingered the money in my pocket. What harm could there be in a few tries—especially after practicing? I had nothing to lose! Who would know the difference?

Cautiously, I approached the rail separating me from the carnival barker. His browned, leathery hands, criss-crossed with huge veins like rabbit warrens, handed me three small, red balls that I was to roll down a slightly sloped board. If I could roll the balls just right, they would stop in the holes totaling 100 and I would win the prize of my choice. If I rolled the balls too vigorously, however, they would bounce over or out of the pockets and I would win nothing. As I surveyed the game and tested the weight of the balls with my hands, I noticed his pale blue, tired eyes staring at me with a mixture of amusement and cynicism. Even with his missing front tooth, thinning gray-black hair plastered to his head, and his thin, poorly clothed body he had a kind of magnetism; I couldn't help but wish I had his confidence, bravado, and devil-may-care attitude.

Vic, as the name on his shirt pocket read, gave me five rounds of practice balls. By the third set of three, I was racking up 100 with ease. "Looks to me like ya got it, girlie," Vic finally drawled. "Time ta play for real. Tell ya what. I'll give ya a deal. I kinda like ya; you're a cute thing. Instead of three balls for a quarter, I'll give ya 15 for a buck."

Before Vic could change his mind, I quickly plunked down the dollar with the realization nagging at me that I had just committed two weeks of hard-earned money. How many trips to the garbage, dishes dried, dogs walked, and babies minded? How many homework assignments completed and lectures by my parents had I endured for that single green bill? But the cost was cheap, compared to the thrill of defying my elders. Besides, the prizes that

caught my eye were worth way more than a dollar. Imagine my grandparents' surprise when I walked in the door with a giant, plush bear or a glittering Cupie doll. Before going home, I'd have to concoct a story of how I ended up with such a prize since I had promised I would avoid the midway.

I handed Vic the money and just as I was about to roll the first ball down the chute, Vic warned me, "Stay behind the red line, kid. See them rules posted there?"

The red line! What red line? But I had just practiced leaning against the railing! "Oh well," I said to myself. "I have fifteen balls. I got the hang of it the last time in that many tries. I'll just use the first six as practice."

It took me less than two minutes to lose my turn and my dollar. As I stood there dazed, Vic's voice interrupted my trance. "Hurry up kid. Move aside. Don't hold up the line. Can't ya see someone else wants a chance?"

As I scurried away like a roach caught in the kitchen at midnight, I could hear my grandparents' warnings ringing in my ears, a list of "morals" meant to induce shame and humiliation for my act of waste and stupidity. I could also hear Vic say to the next sucker in a conspiratorial tone, "Hey honey. How about giving the ball a roll?"

◇ **ABOUT THE AUTHOR**

Susan Bennett teaches English at Humboldt State University. She taught junior high English in La Puente, California before returning to Berkeley for her Ph.D. Susan has two daughters, and lives near Eureka, California with chickens, ducks, a goat, a blue heeler, a hedgehog, and a couple of horses. She is the director of the Redwood Writing Project.

◇ **NOTES FROM THE AUTHOR**

I've often wondered why I recall some events so clearly and others are dim memories. Those events that stick are the ones I like to write about because sometimes they lead to powerful revelations. Through the process of writing I come to see how an event helped shape the person I am now. I think I remember the episode in "Crossing the Line" well because I finally realized that maybe my grandparents were responding to their own bad experiences and not just trying to stop me from having a good time. Like most adolescents, I was sure I knew more than my elders and that I could take care of myself. I didn't believe anything bad could happen to me. Now that I have teenagers of my own, I realize that mistakes can be costly and, as adults, we would like to save our children from learning the hard way.

One of the problems I had writing this story was trying to capture not only the generation gap between me and my grandparents, but also the cultural differences between an American-born adolescent and immigrants. Both of my grandparents came to the United States when they were the same age I was when I stayed with them. They had to learn quickly to survive in their new country; this experience made both of them anxious throughout their lives. They were always self-conscious about the way they spoke English and distrusted American customs. I still don't think I was successful showing their lack of confidence without making them seem stern or dumb, and I was unable to accurately represent the way they spoke.

◇ **WRITING CHALLENGE: EXPERIMENT WITH POINT OF VIEW**

Think of a time when you defied your parents' rules or wishes because you thought they were mean or stupid, and they turned out to be right. Did you get caught? What did you learn from the experience? Did you develop a new respect or a different attitude about their intentions? Try to write about the event from the adults' point of view to gain additional perspective. Later, try to write about this incident showing its effect on you—how you became more mature and/or aware of your vulnerability.

THE CAT WHO BECAME A RABBIT

One evening when I was thirteen, I answered a knock at the door. A nervous-looking woman stood there, wringing her hands,

"Oh, I am so sorry!" she wailed.

"About what?"

She motioned to the street. "Those kids told me the cat was yours. I hit your cat. With my car. If you could give me a towel and a box—oh, it just ran out in front of me, and I couldn't stop!" Tears flowed down her cheeks. My first thought was, What a nice lady.

Then I had a sinking feeling for the cat. Well, of course, the cat had been hit. It happened to the best of them. We had lost so many cats by now I almost couldn't keep track. There were yellow ones, white ones, a black one with a resounding purr. Our most recent previous cat had been swept down the sewer during a rainstorm, caught up in a swirling current, the kind that turns streets into rivers. Calling for it from our front porch between thunderclaps, I had actually seen it vanish down the drain. There was nothing we could do, except keep our cats indoors all the time, and the cats we knew didn't like that. One of our cats had even frozen in the snow, and we tried to thaw it out in the oven.

My parents had gathered at the front door by now, and my brother emerged from his room. I told the lady it was okay; she didn't mean to hit it. She cried harder. She acted as if she wanted us to have a funeral for the cat right then and there. We were all consoling the woman who had hit our cat. I think my father even offered her coffee. She shook her head and left, and we gingerly carried the box to the backyard.

And then we felt very sad. Because it had been a cute and mischievous cat, and it would never stand on its hind legs for a taste of peanut butter again.

About an hour later, I heard another knock on the door. Flinging it open (no one was afraid to open doors in those days), I found the same woman, the cat-hitter, with an absolutely HUGE white rabbit in her arms. She held it out to me. "This is for you," she said. "I raise New Zealand Angoras and this is to take the place of your cat." There was no question mark in her voice.

I felt stunned. What an interesting proposition. Was it even possible?

Never in my life had I considered having a rabbit. It seemed as unlikely as having a giraffe. I was a little afraid to take it from her. Did rabbits bite? It was five times the size of the cat that had died. Did fingers look like carrots?

Again my parents and brother gathered around the door, startled to see our new family member. My mother reached out a tentative hand. "So soft!" The woman seemed in a hurry now. She had made her decision, paid her penance, and was ready never to see us again. As she fled down the driveway, I called out, "But what does it EAT? Does it like to sleep indoors or out?"

"Build a hutch!" she said. "With screens! In your backyard!"

Our father was groaning.

Because he was a Palestinian refugee, he had lost many things in his life already—his home, all his family's money in the bank, his friends. People he

knew had lost lentil fields, olive trees, whole villages. It was a little hard to complain about, say, losing our ice cream money, or even our cat, when we knew what other people were going through elsewhere.

He often said to us, "Your pets get treated better than many people in the world."

We let our new rabbit sleep in our garage in a laundry basket that first night. Later I let it sleep in a drawer in my room. I just opened the drawer and it jumped in and curled up on top of my clothes. We bought rabbit chow at a pet store. We cut apples into bite-size pieces. Later, after our father found a hutch at a neighbor's garage sale, the rabbit started living a penned-up life in the backyard, though we always let it out to hop around and brought it into the house when it was cold.

Right at the brink of my own first glimmers of romantic interest (I had just been kissed by a boy at a movie theater and was still in shock), I took the rabbit to meet another rabbit for the sake of breeding. I knew nothing about these things and didn't know how long it would take. Two minutes? Twenty hours? The serious boy at the other rabbit's house assured me I could take my own rabbit home after an hour.

I wonder now what made me imagine I suddenly needed nine rabbits when just a moment before, I had never had any.

The babies were adorable. My girlfriends came over from school to play with them. They sat in a circle on the floor and held them. I was very popular for about three months. One evening, as we were eating supper in our backyard at the picnic table, with cozy rabbits hopping all around us, my father and mother startled us with an idea. Would we like to move overseas? Meet our Arab grandmother? Learn another language? Turn our lives upside down?

"I thought they are always fighting over there," my brother said.

I stared at my dazzling pets. Some were white like their mother. Some were cocoa and midnight. I could never convince my parents to let me take nine rabbits in an airplane.

We packed up everything. We sold what we couldn't pack. Reluctantly, I gave my ravenous rabbits to a very cute boy named Bob Finley, who had a large yard, and whom I had hoped I might be kissing one day, sooner rather than later. Now I would never know.

Before we boarded the plane in New York City to fly across the ocean to the Holy Land, which seemed still on the path to becoming truly holy, to becoming a place where people of all stripes and faiths could live together in harmony, before we embarked on the vast adventure that would change our lives forever, I called Bob Finley long-distance to see how the rabbits were doing.

He sounded shocked to hear from me. His voice crackled with concern. "Oh gee," he said. "I really hate to tell you this. I didn't think you would call. I thought I wouldn't have to…"

"WHAT? WHAT? WHAT?" I demanded.

"Well, you know that German shepherd I have? Ernie? That big yellow one? Well…"

Ernie had eaten all nine of my precious rabbits in a swoop. They were lunch. They were dinner. Ernie had overturned the hutch by himself and unlatched the screen.

"I feel terrible about it," Bob Finley said.

Well, sure he did. I hung up the phone very quietly, a lump in my throat. How cuddly they had been. How trusting, the little babies… I wondered whether or not to tell my family right then. It seemed a dubious omen to pass on this sorrowful news right before flying across the dark ocean.

I stared out into the winking lights of a New York night. We kids who knew only one world would soon know another. People and animals who had good luck would also have bad. The cat who became a rabbit, then nine rabbits, had now become a dog.

◇ ABOUT THE AUTHOR

Naomi Shihab Nye was born in St. Louis and now lives in downtown San Antonio, Texas, with her photographer husband and their golf-playing son. They also have a cat named Scout whom they hope will remain a cat as long as possible. Everyone in her family writes in a personal notebook every day. Over the years she has visited hundreds of different schools to talk about reading and writing with students of all ages. She likes to see the student work that different schools hang up in their hallways.

◇ NOTES FROM THE AUTHOR

In some ways I have been writing stories from my childhood all my life—in poems, picture books, essays, and a novel or two. I used to say that I loved my childhood so much I would never get over it—now it seems I was telling the truth. How is it possible to keep pulling so many buckets of water out of the same well? It wasn't that everything in childhood was so easy for me or anything—on the contrary, our family was fraught with the usual troubles that many families have—worry about money, parents not always getting along, mixed-culture conflicts, depression, and so on. But I loved that world. I loved it with all my heart, and there is nothing I like better than going back to it in writing now, finding new connections, seeing new glimmers of light among those trees.

What makes those early days and streets and characters feel so vivid? It's as if all my senses were continually on high alert, soaking in experiences, storing up smells and sounds and infinitesimal details. I used to worry about growing older because I thought I might forget all those precious days. Writing has helped them stay alive.

When I go back to those streets and neighborhoods in real life now (in reality they have changed very little), I often wonder—am I remembering what really happened? Am I remembering something I wrote? Even when we think we are writing nonfiction, there's a tantalizing element of invention involved—*how* we remember something becomes its own intriguing fiction.

◇ ON EDITING

One of the hardest things about writing a story or poem is knowing where it begins and ends. Often we include extra material in our first draft of any story, but we shouldn't worry too much about that, because we can always cut it out later.

This story, for example, originally opened with some background details about my father and his coming to the United States as a college student. I wanted to give a little history about our family, to place our cats into a context.

But Bob Sizoo read the story and thought it really started on the second page and suggested I cut out the first page. He said the first part moved too slowly and made it seem as if my story was more about loss, than what happened next.

Such suggestions are not shocking to me anymore—I have been writing a long time and appreciate how important such changes can be. We should try our best to feel receptive when other people—teachers, editors, friends—suggest changes, though of course, sometimes we have a little instinct to defend our own ideas, and we don't have to do what other people say. On the following page is the original part of my story that was cut off. I tried to pull a little of the information into the current draft. Do you think I did the right thing?

Deleted Beginning

Because our father was a Palestinian refugee, my brother and I heard many stories about people losing things as we grew up. It was a little bit hard to complain about, say, losing our ice cream money, when we knew what other people were going through in the world.

We lived in a small square house in the middle of the United States, and we had a cat. We always had a cat. A yellow or a white one. A black one with a resounding purr. We preferred solid colors though we, ourselves, were ethnically rather striped. We had street cats, not fancy cats. They lived both inside and out. They had access to the dark mysterious night. We did minor, safe experiments with them: Would a cat eat mashed potatoes? I loved to have a cat curled on the end of my bed. Our father was never as excited about having a cat as we were. He said the cat got treated better than many people in the world.

Our father's family had lost their own house in the Old City of Jerusalem and all their money in the bank when Israel was created in 1948. Other people had lost lentil fields, olive trees, and whole villages. Too bad the Jews and Arabs couldn't just have cooperated from the beginning and found a way to live side by side.

Our father's best friend had been killed in Jerusalem while the two of them were sitting on a bench together, but he wouldn't discuss that. Our mother told us. All these accumulating sadnesses in his country made our father apply for a college scholarship and get on a boat, leaving his own crying mother, traveling far to see what was over the horizon.

We were. We were over the horizon. In just a few years, our father would be married to an American, and we would be born. His new world would contain cozy tree-lined neighborhoods and cars and school bells and rolled-up newspapers pitched into front yards. Grocery stores sold 20 kinds of bread. His kids would ride bicycles and dress like monsters for Halloween. It was an easier world than the one he had grown up in, and sometimes he let us know that, but not too often. Our easy-going dad rarely got mad and told better jokes and stories than the other dads we knew, so we felt lucky.

◇ NOTES FROM THE EDITOR

I have never met Naomi and she is obviously a fine writer. I felt a little strange asking her to leave out a big chunk at the beginning of the piece, especially since that chunk was really well written. I especially liked the sentence, "We did minor, safe experiments with them: would a cat eat mashed potatoes?" But I thought the story was more inviting or attention-getting when it began with the lady coming to the door nervously wringing her hands, and left out a little of the family history. Naomi is a confident enough writer so she knows that my advice was intended to make her fine story even stronger—that I was not criticizing her as a person or even as a writer. The odd part is that I could have been wrong. Maybe you, the audience, would have liked it better before. There is always a certain element of mystery in writing.

◇ WRITING CHALLENGE: WRITE ABOUT A TRANSFORMATION

This is a story about transformations. Think of something in your childhood that transformed into something else. Did a holiday that started out to be sad ever surprise you by turning into a won-

derful one? Did a "hard teacher" become the favorite teacher you ever had? Did an enemy turn into a friend?

Many times a loss may be closely bound to a new discovery. Your grandparents die—and you start seeing other old people who aren't even related to you in a different way. A friend moves away—and suddenly something you shared becomes more important.

On the other hand, the transformation might be very small—something that no one notices but you. A sense of bravery. A new dream. It might be a transformation in the way that you look at something.

Write about one you have experienced. Don't worry too much about where the story begins. Write freely and generously. Then go back to it in an hour or a day later and see if there are whole chunks you could do without. See if you can find the real, essential story, inside the larger story. If you are working on a computer, be sure to save different drafts, too.

Have fun! Explore it! Don't feel you have to have an exact idea for the ending when you begin writing! The words will lead you as they unfold.

Also try this: In the first paragraph of "The Cat Who Became a Rabbit," Naomi Shihab Nye was faced with a woman wringing her hands and terribly distressed. Apparently she was more upset about running over Naomi's cat than Naomi was about losing it. Naomi felt worse about the woman's pain than she did losing her cat. She'd lost lots of cats.

Sometimes stories that seem terrible to a character within the story or to the reader are seen as odd or as a learning experience to another character. For example, I wrote a story about my mom dying. She had cancer for nine years, and at the time of her death, she was ready to go, and I had prepared myself for her leaving. The climax of the story features the last conversation I had with her. When I read it aloud to my peers, they often cry. But I don't see the story as sad. It's really about celebrating having the time to say good-bye.

Write about a time when you or a character in your story learned something interesting or felt curious about something that another character was sad or upset about. Or, do the opposite. Write about an incident that some characters thought was funny or entertaining and you or another character thought was sad, serious or embarrassing.

SEW WHAT

◇◇◇◇◇◇◇◇◇◇◇◇◇◇◇◇◇

The summer after seventh grade my mother signed me up for sewing lessons at the Singer Sewing Center in downtown Gary. The teacher's name was Mrs. Heart. She had shiny glasses and her blue eyes seemed brightly magnified behind them.

On the first day of class, Mrs. Heart instructed us to undress down to our slips. In 1959 well-raised girls wore skirts and dresses when we went uptown. There wasn't a day that was too hot for a full slip with bra, panties, and a garter belt or girdle to hold up our stockings. The stockings came in colors like red fox and brown sugar. We put them on carefully, one at a time.

Mrs. Heart told us to partner up to measure each other. "To make a properly fitting garment, you must have accurate measurements and then select the correct pattern size, girls," she said.

No one chose me, so the petite instructor reached up and gingerly wrapped the tape measure around different parts of my body. "My favorite time to sew," she said, as she wrapped the cloth tape measure around my waist, "is when the house is quiet and I turn on the FM station."

"I love to listen to the radio, too," I replied. For a moment, I forgot the embarrassment that everyone had been chosen to be a partner but me as I was the only black girl in the class.

On the radio I listened to rock and roll, rhythm and blues, baseball, and the news, and on our long drives south to visit my mama's family in Georgia, country tunes and twangy Appalachian church services crackled from the dash through the night. There were long stretches when Dad knew not to get off of the road. We tried to keep the gas tank full, and we carried our own food and water.

Our annual trip to Georgia was a memory by now; I had more immediate concerns. "Just relax, dear," said Mrs. Heart, measuring my waist, "if you hold your breath now, the garment won't fit later."

"Look who's being measured by the teacher," one girl stage whispered to Amanda Clark, the most popular girl in my seventh-grade class. Amanda had silky blond hair, a little ski-jump nose like a model's, and more boyfriends than she could handle.

In an even louder whisper, Amanda replied, "I know *I* wouldn't want to measure *her.*" I pretended not to hear and tried to relax. If sewing class was going to be like this, I at least wanted my clothes to fit.

In our little house in Gary, it seemed that Mama worked all the time. "A lady is polished and refined. She has academic, social, and homemaking skill," Mama would say, as she helped me thread the bobbin at night when I practiced my sewing. Sewing was serious business. While she washed clothes, ironed, or cooked, she'd tell us our family had four generations of excellent seamstresses. A simple talent like sewing had translated to advantage. Even the smallest bit of status made a big difference during that terrible time long ago.

Her papa was a hell-raiser. On the railroad he was a lantern man, a switcher, and a signaler. Grandpapa worked on the rail lines from Columbus, Georgia, to Columbus, Ohio. He brought home barrels of fine china with silverware, bolts of fabric for dresses, knickers, and curtains, bedspreads, pillowcases, tablecloths. He brought back boxes of pencils and reams of paper. "My chillun will get an education!" Mama told us her papa used to say. She was proud that he valued knowledge more than anything.

As a boy of seven, he plowed cotton behind a mule and dreamed of sitting in a classroom. "He had a mind like a steel trap," Mama would say. He'd wait beside the road for the children who could go to school to pass by on their way home. Her papa would ask them to stop and show him, in the dust, what they had learned that day. He learned the alphabet this way and how to do arithmetic. For years I thought that the privileged children, the ones who did get to go to school, must have been white. One day, as Mama told the story, I asked her, "Weren't the schoolchildren white?" She explained that even some colored children were better off than the barefoot tenant farmer boy.

He wanted to get out of sharecropping even more than he wanted an education. Very little had changed during the late 1800s when my mama's papa was a boy. Poor people belonged to the land, and the land belonged to the owners.

"Papa was just off the edge of slavery," Aunt Kate would say.

"Big Mama Katherine was a little girl about three when freedom was declared," my mama told us.

On our family trips south each summer, I'd think about my relatives and their long roots growing into the Georgia clay. When we went south on the train, I asked my mama about the Mason-Dixon line and watched the horizon and thick green countryside for signs of change. What was it? Where was it?

I looked for that mysterious line that divided America. They taught us in school that the Confederacy lost the war; the Union was saved, and when Abraham Lincoln freed the slaves, all men truly became equal.

The trains stopped in Kentucky or Tennessee to switch engines, and to take on and let off passengers. We arrived in Georgia and filed from the rear cars through the gates marked "colored" into the waiting room set aside for us.

Questioning the mores of the South was considered impolite. But I continued asking about the signs on the fountain and bathrooms, restaurants, the movie theater entrances, libraries, and parks. People like us had stopped going to most public places since it was against the law to be there.

"That's just the way they do things down here," my aunts explained when I would not be put off. In downtown Albany I drank water from a white-only fountain. No one called the police or seemed to notice. For a moment, in 1960, I was a disobedient civilian, a freedom rider, a demonstrator sitting in, too young, before my time.

Back home in Gary, I attended my sewing class. It wasn't "Whites only," but it almost was. After the fifth class, Mrs. Heart told us that we would enter the garment we made in a contest at the end of the summer. We decided that I'd make a three-piece suit and chose a heavy woven cotton fabric for the skirt and jacket—a dark brown paisley print. The round-necked sleeveless blouse was of the same material in a deep shade of gold. I made a gold velveteen cloach hat. It had tucks, a flexible brim, and a covered button on the crown. I lined the skirt, the jacket, and the hat.

None of the girls ever did talk to me. Mrs. Heart answered my questions and showed me the finer points of clipping and understitching facings so that they laid flat and smooth. She was my permanent partner that summer, the only one who would come near me when we tried on our skirts and measured for hemlines.

I went home and practiced making slip stitches that were tiny and invisible. I listened to my dad's radio. He had FM and I liked Beethoven and Charlie Parker and Bach and Chopin and John Coltrane. Mrs. Heart's quiet patience and the music made me feel better, more human, and not a pariah, though I wondered why the other girls would not come near me.

The three-piece suit with matching velveteen hat was quite an ensemble. Our entries were identified by number and placed in categories by age. Mama picked me up that final afternoon.

We went back that night to hear the judges' decisions. The garments were on dress racks in the back room of the store. The tables along the walls were empty. Our scraps and hopes had been stitched together, pressed open, trimmed, and hemmed. They hung neatly on hangers.

We sat together, mother and daughter, sort of huddled as I recall. I shivered a little bit, though the Indiana August night was warm. Folding chairs were in rows, making the Singer Sewing Center look like a storefront church prepared for revival. I know the winner would model her creation at another Singer store, maybe in Hammond or even Chicago.

My baby, the only Negro, Mama thought, when they announced my name in second place. Second was good. How could I have modeled my suit and hat in front of all those white-only, blue-eyed people looking down at and through me as if surprised that I had the nerve to exist? The stare was the same. I knew it from both sides of the mysterious Mason-Dixon line.

"And the first-place winner is Amanda Clark," gushed the manager of the Singer Sewing Center. Amanda's family had flowers for her. The other girls crowded around. Mama and I went in back to get my outfit. A few girls paused or stepped aside near the racks, getting their also-rans.

I carried the soft, heavy cotton suit across my two arms. The entry number and second-place ribbon dangled from the sleeve of the jacket. As we neared the door, Mrs. Heart approached my mama and me. "I just wanted to commend you on what a good job your daughter did this summer. It wasn't easy for her. She is a poised young lady and an excellent dressmaker."

"Why thank you," Mama replied graciously. "She's a fourth-generation seamstress, you know. But she really appreciates all she learned from you this summer. Don't you, dear?" Mama looked at me.

"Yes, Mrs. Heart, I do," I replied sincerely.

Mrs. Heart shuffled a little, looked at the floor for a moment, then looked up directly in Mama's eyes. "The judges gave her first place until they found out she's colored." Mama was more than surprised. I thought about walls and signs in Georgia.

The first-place winner looked at her simple shirt-waist dress in the mirror. It had a covered belt, no hat, no style even from across the room. "So what?" I asked myself, as I digested Mrs. Heart's revelation.

"Do tell!" Aunt Kate used to say. "You hush." I knew that I had outsewed them all. They'd had to cheat. Anyone who needs to rig a contest must be fairly inferior and insecure, I decided.

There was a minor defeat and a small victory in September of 1960 in downtown Gary, Indiana. A girl who had been cruel and racist toward me for three months won first place in a crooked contest. What did she win? What did I gain?

Some days I turn on my FM radio, pin down a pattern, and cut out a garment, and I wonder about Mrs. Heart. Every day I look at the pictures of Mama and Grandmother and think about my forebears and their days in Georgia.

◇ ABOUT THE AUTHOR

Kay Carter teaches kindergarten and first grade in Oakland, California. She has four adult children, is a church pianist, and has been in education for 30 years. Kay has kept a daily journal for 25 years, and wrote her first poem, which she remembers to this day, at age eight.

◇ NOTES FROM THE AUTHOR

When I began writing this autobiographical incident, I knew two things: I knew that I wanted to write about my childhood and early teen years. And I wanted to write about the South.

The incident occurred in the Midwest, "up north," as the old folks used to say, in Indiana, not Down South in Georgia. I found myself with two ideas. The challenge was to find all of the ways that the two ideas were related. I had to weave them together.

As I worked on the piece, I realized that the two ideas were equally important. From living in the South as well as the North, I had experiences with many forms of racism, and my autobiographical vignette was focused on a similar experience I had in the Midwest.

My challenge then was to write about the two ideas with balance. Most of the decisions I made were about balance and choice of detail. I tried to tell enough of the right details about each place to enable readers to visualize the times I was writing about, my feelings and thoughts as I grew up in the two areas.

I am a teacher, and it is difficult not to over explain. My readers will tell me whether they were sufficiently informed and clear about times and people and places. Whether there was room for discovery of pleasant or unpleasant surprises.

I worked through a process, choosing details that balance both structure and content in hope that the story would be able to stand on its own.

◇ WRITING CHALLENGE: WRITE ABOUT PLAYING FAIR

Finish this sentence: "It's not whether you win or lose, but how you…" This is one of the most universal adages in American culture. Long before my little league coach introduced me to this phrase, it had been drummed into me in school and at home. Playing fair is more important than winning. Kay Carter's story features a girl who lost a contest because the contest was rigged. She knew that she had made a wonderful suit, and took pride in her work. Regardless of the outcome of the contest, she had "played the game" fairly.

Write about an incident in your life in which it was more important to play fair than to win, or write about a time when you or someone you know paid more attention to winning than to playing fair.

First-hand
Biographical Sketches

THE CUT ANCHOR LINE

◇◇◇◇◇◇◇◇◇◇◇◇◇◇◇◇◇◇◇

Not many things irritated Uncle Nelson. He had no edges so to speak. Republican relatives might get a rise out of him and make him spit more emphatically. Cut anchor lines, however, brought more than spit.

Uncle Nelson ran a boat business renting boats he built himself. They were heavy and durable enough to withstand the ignorance of city people. He never lost a customer to the sea. Occasionally a good blow might come up from the southeast and the inexperienced fisherman couldn't buck the head wind with two men rowing. They'd pull the boat up on the west shore and walk their equipment across land and then tell Uncle Nelson how impossible the conditions were in the face of such a sea.

Uncle Nelson either waited for the wind to shift, or if he needed the boat sooner, sculled the skiff around the point against the head wind himself. That meant he'd place one oar in a small half-moon cut in the stern and propel the skiff straight into the head wind with the simple back and forth motion of one oar. It took me five years to learn how to scull a boat half the size when the water was flat calm.

On the planking above the bow of the boat and on signs posted around the boathouse, Uncle Nelson advertised what to do if a fisherman got his anchor stuck on the bottom. Experienced fisherman knew how to row in a circle in order to pull the anchor from different directions. This usually dislodged the anchor, which looked like a large grappling hook.

The anchors cost seven dollars each, which was big money in the 1940s. Boat rentals were a dollar fifty a day on weekdays and two dollars on weekends. Uncle Nelson purchased his anchors from an old, eighty-seven-year-old blacksmith friend, Mr. Spooner, in the center of Fairhaven. He was the only blacksmith left in the Fairhaven/New Bedford area. Uncle Nelson thought that "any day now that old man will keel over, and I'll be without anchors." Uncle Nelson was eighty-three himself.

If the anchors wouldn't budge from the bottom, the signs instructed the fishermen to throw out the rest of the anchor line, along with the buoy attached to the end of it. The buoys were painted gray and stamped with Uncle Nelson's initial HNW. When the fisherman returned without his anchor, he told Uncle Nelson where the buoy was located; when the weather calmed, and the buoy could be seen more easily, he sculled out and pulled the anchor himself.

Uncle Nelson could even forgive men who didn't understand the directions and failed to toss the buoy. They'd arrive at the boathouse and say, "We couldn't pull the anchor, so we cut the line." Usually, they arrived, line in hand, to show Uncle Nelson how much rope they'd saved. "I reached as far down into the water as I could, and then I cut the line," the man would report in an air of generosity. Uncle Nelson's response was a grunt and an "alright, put the line over there."

Several times each season some slicker from out of state told an outright lie. My brother and I worked for Uncle Nelson, collecting money, cleaning boats, and hauling them up with the old Buick for the night. We checked each boat when it came in to see that oars, anchor, and lines were all present when collecting the money. Most people told us when an anchor was lost, even the ones who errantly cut the line. The worst didn't and had to be taught Uncle Nelson style.

"Sir, there doesn't seem to be an anchor here."

"Oh that. Uh, the anchor line broke." The man pointed to the severed line, cut cleanly across, a straight end with no dangling fibers.

Uncle Nelson looked at the unblinking man who, unfortunately, may have made a habit of telling untruths. "Come with me, my boy," Uncle Nelson gestured with a long finger. "Come up here and I'll show you something."

At the top of the boat runway was a post with some old, used line Uncle Nelson kept for such moments. "Watch what I do and what happens." Uncle Nelson threw two half hitches around the post and another two half hitches around the bumper of the old Buick. While the man watched impatiently, wondering what the crazy old man had in mind, Uncle Nelson put the Buick in reverse. The line snapped instantly.

Uncle Nelson glided out of the seat and picked up the snapped line and brought it to the man. "You say your line broke. This line just broke off this post here. Now here is yours and here is the one that just snapped when I backed the car up. How are they different?" The man stood staring at the ground, not at the line, and said nothing.

"When a line snaps, there are two short and one long strand just like this one." Uncle Nelson then waved the cut line instructor-like and spoke directly at the man. "You cut yours with a knife... only way you can get a clean slice like the one you got. I've lost an anchor, but worse, you've lost your character. I won't be lied to and that'll cost you $10.00, $7.00 for the anchor and $3.00 for the line. And I don't give a damn if you ever come back."

The man paid; they always did. Strangely, the ones who lied were usually well-to-do with fancy tackle boxes, poles, and clothes. They didn't think the old man at the shore could understand the ways of the sophisticated. Natives viewed Uncle Nelson differently. When they sensed one of those liars was in trouble with the old man, they'd just gather around and take in the drama.

◇ **ABOUT THE AUTHOR**

Don Graves has been a teacher, school principal, and a language supervisor for a city school system. He is professor emeritus at the University of New Hampshire and lives with his wife Betty near the windiest place in North America. He is the author of many books, including *A Fresh Look at Writing; Baseball, Snakes, and Summer Squash;* and *The Energy to Teach.*

◇ **NOTES FROM THE AUTHOR**

Uncle Nelson taught through demonstration. Although his demonstrations were directed toward the person who needed teaching, in this case the man who lied about the anchor line, my brother and I caught the full impact of the event. We have carried that story about the meaning of honesty throughout our lives.

I often wonder how many teaching stories are lost when a business owner says, "Ah, that's just a write-off. I see customers like that all the time." What is the effect on the witnesses?

About the piece. This was a story that I'd told many, many times before I actually wrote it. That's a lot different than taking a vague memory and creating a piece. So, in one sense it was an easy one to put down. As you can tell, it is very oral. Much of the flavor of the boats and the men who were there is in it.

◇ **NOTES FROM THE EDITOR**

I'm always intimidated by suggesting improvements to the work of good writers. In the case of Don Graves, whose books have arguably done more to improve the way teachers teach writing than any other author in America, intimidation isn't a strong enough word. After reading his first draft, I thought, Who am I to suggest changes to *him*? Even so, I realize that every writer has rough spots and questions about his or her writing. One of my questions was about his use of the word *glided* when Uncle Nelson got out of the truck. I pictured Uncle Nelson as strong and competent, but not necessarily graceful, so the word bothered me. He wrote back the following:

About the word "glided" that you mentioned about Uncle Nelson getting out of the truck. Everything he did appeared effortless and was a glide. Note that in my piece about him in How to Catch a Shark *that he could take his right foot and scratch his left ear, or that he could kick the top of a doorjamb. He was so loose and flexible, a metaphor for his life.*

But, as you pointed out in your response, there are some oral elements that just don't work and need to be changed.

After rereading the story, I realized that Uncle Nelson needed grace and balance to scull the rowboat across the choppy sea, and that a careful reader would think the word *glided* was appropriate.

I mentioned this for two reasons. First, it shows how much thought and struggle can go into the choice of a single word. Second, I was curious what you as readers and listeners thought about the word. Did you notice it as you went through the story? Do you think we made a good decision to leave it in?

◇ **WRITING CHALLENGE: WRITE ABOUT SOMEONE TAKING A STAND**

Try to retrieve an event when your father, mother, friend, or relative took a stand for what he or she thought was right. Tell the story of that occasion. Take no more than ten minutes to write a crude version of that story. Change nothing; just say it! Fix it later.

MY HERO

◇◇◇◇◇◇◇◇◇◇◇◇◇◇◇◇◇◇◇◇

Ordinarily, Brandon's father drank cheap whiskey from a half-pint bottle in a paper bag, but the day his first child was born he knew he could talk Ray the bartender into a couple double shots of Jack Daniel's.

"This better be for real this time, Butch" Ray said. "Last time you hit me up for a free drink you said you were getting married; you're no more married to Judy than I am."

"Yeah, but you got a good laugh out of it," Brandon's father replied. "Anyway, you seen how big Judy was last week."

"Knowing you, she was wearing a pillow."

Ray's words echoed in Butch's worried and slightly spinning head as he left the Alley Cat and walked the three blocks to the hospital. "I wish she was wearing a pillow," he thought as he strode to the information desk in the lobby. "Where's the babies kept?" he asked.

"Maternity's on the third floor," the clerk replied.

After receiving directions from the third floor nurse stationed outside the elevator, Butch wandered into Room 362. "What's up, Judy?" he asked. Judy slurped the last sip of water from the foam cup in her hand, slowly removed the bent straw from her cracked lips, and swallowed. Her always bloodshot eyes seemed redder than normal and the deep creases in her face rose slightly as she squinted back at Butch.

"Where you been?" Judy asked.

"Out."

"Well I had the baby three hours ago, and I want out of here." Drops of sweat appeared on Judy's forehead. She hadn't had any meth in almost eighteen hours, and she was beginning to shake slightly.

"Where's the baby?" asked Butch.

Judy's puffy eyes narrowed. "You want to see the baby? Oh, we'll go see the baby. 'Nurse, nurse,'" she yelled at the nurse in the hallway.

"Yes?" responded Nurse Rosa.

"We want to see our baby, now."

Rosa led Judy and Butch to the nursery. "Stand out here and look in through the window," she ordered. "I'll hold him up for you."

They watched as Rosa inspected the tag at the end of the cradle, gently slid her hand under the blanket, and lifted the baby to her chest. As Rosa walked toward the window, Brandon's parents could see a red, splotchy face above the edge of his blanket.

"He's kinda cute," Butch said.

"Yeah, right," Judy wiped her cuff against her running nose. Holding the edge of the blanket, the nurse looked at Judy. Judy smirked and nodded. The nurse slowly folded back the blanket. Brandon lay exposed to his parents' view.

Butch's eyes widened, "Oh my God," he said. Brandon's right arm ended just below the elbow. His left arm stopped above where the elbow belonged. His left leg ended barely below the knee, and his right leg was just an incomplete femur. Butch turned to Judy, "I need a drink."

"Me, too," said Judy, "let's get out of here." She put on her best smile of thanks for Nurse Rosa on the other side of the window. They walked back toward the room and stopped an orderly in the hallway.

"Excuse me," Butch asked in his most sober and polite voice. "My wife would like a Coke. Could you tell us where the cafeteria is?"

"Second floor."

"Thanks," he smiled. In the elevator, without a word, he pushed "G" for the ground floor. Butch

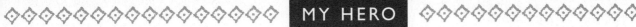

and Judy walked out of the hospital and never returned.

* * * * * * *

Almost 12 years later, I called Brandon's name from my sixth-grade roll sheet on the first day of school. "I'm here, but I don't want to be," he answered. The other students laughed tentatively, wondering about my response as I glanced up at Brandon. He glared back at me with his best mean look, but he couldn't hide the pleasure he felt in giving his teacher the first pop quiz of the year. Brandon had started at Lincoln School the previous year and his fifth-grade teacher had told me he doesn't like people feeling sorry for him; he wants to be treated like everyone else. I knew this was my first test.

"Well, I guess you're stuck here, just like the rest of us," I replied with a smile.

"I guess so," he laughed, unable to retain his tough-guy demeanor.

After living through two adoptions and three foster families, Brandon had become a tester. You couldn't fake him out. "Why do we have to know this?" he'd ask. You couldn't lie to him, and if you told him something was important, you'd better mean it. If you weren't sincere, he'd hone in like a laser beam and do surgery on your conscience. His attitude said, After all I've been through, I don't have time to waste on something that's not going to help me. I had to agree.

If Brandon disrupted class, he'd take his licks. He'd never say, "What did I do?" or "I didn't do anything," when he broke one of the class rules, as he often did. "You're right, Mr. Sizoo," he'd reluctantly admit when I kept him after school, "I messed up."

But he'd get downright belligerent if he felt I was being unfair to another student. One day I thought a girl named Julie threw an eraser at the boy across the table from her. "Julie, I need to talk to you for a minute at lunch," I calmly said.

"What did she do?" Brandon yelled. He swung his stainless steel legs out from behind the desk and rocked his torso backward. "She didn't do anything," he bellowed, swinging forward and up onto his Nike-shod rubber feet. "You don't have the right to accuse her; she didn't do anything." Brandon began to walk toward me.

"Okay, okay," I said, "I haven't called the police yet or anything."

"I threw the eraser," Melissa, the girl next to Julie, said sheepishly.

"Okay," I responded, turning to Melissa, "may I talk to *you* for a minute at lunch?"

"Yeah, sure" she replied.

I turned to Brandon, "Well, you got your client off. I hope you don't plan to charge her too much for your legal services."

"No, that time it was free." Brandon turned toward his seat. "But next time it'll cost her."

After that event, I began to call him Esquire Brandon, out of respect for what I thought could be his future career in law. Several times through the year, Brandon defended someone he felt was being treated unfairly, whether it was someone in the class, in the news, or even some historical figure. He knew what it was like to be abused.

Brandon was frequently in trouble. When he got mad, he used language that would make a logger blush, and one time I barely got to him and another student as they headed to the park after school to fight. I brought them back into the classroom and began talking to Brandon's potential opponent. "Brandon suckered you into a fight, didn't he?"

"No, he called me names and said bad things about my family, and when I got mad *he* said we should fight, not me. He kept saying he could beat me up. I had to fight him."

"Yep. He suckered you into a fight," I said, careful not to look at Brandon.

"What do you mean?"

"Let's say you get to the park and step toward him

with a big right-handed roundhouse, but stumble forward into his swinging stump. He connects with your jaw and knocks you out. Who wins the fight?"

"He does, but that's not going to happen." I sneaked a glance at Brandon. He wore his best bored look. I returned my attention to his potential foe.

"Probably not. But if you beat him up, then everybody will say, 'Big deal, you beat up a guy with no arms.' You see, this is how Brandon suckered you. He knows you can't win." I eventually looked over at Brandon. He looked back at me and finally cracked a grin.

Brandon refused to be seen as handicapped. One day he rushed into our classroom when he arrived at school. "Mr. Sizoo, guess what?" he said, and without waiting for a reply continued, "I'm getting longer legs next month. The doctor measured me and said I'm growing and I need longer legs."

"Really?" I replied curiously.

"Yeah, he said if I had regular legs, I'd be five foot eight. That's tall for my age, isn't it?"

"That's taller than I was at twelve," I commented. He smiled proudly. Throughout the day, he bragged to his classmates about his increasing height.

Brandon tried everything. He played handball at recess, limping on his steel legs, and striking the ball with his shortened arms. He'd hit the red rubber ball once or twice, get out, and get back in line

to try again. He refused to use the artificial hands the state bought him, partly, I think, because he had a bad temper and knew he could really hurt someone with steel hooks for hands. He wrote and drew with a pencil tucked into the crook of his one elbow. The end of that arm extended three inches beyond the elbow and ended in a blunt point. With this point he would type his stories on a keyboard and use a mouse to draw pictures.

Brandon was absent one day near the end of the school year when we were studying Greek mythology. The discussion led to modern-day heroes, mostly sports figures, musicians, astronauts, and relatives of students. I told the class that I have a new hero— Brandon. After all, heroes face all kinds of adversity and show the strength and courage to persevere against enormous odds—to keep trying when the rest of us mere mortals would have given up. I thought that pretty well described Brandon. They agreed.

The next day Brandon returned to school. He noticed me in the classroom during lunch, and walked in. "I heard you told the class I was your hero," he said.

"Yep, that's what I told 'em," I answered.

"That's cool," he said casually, and walked out to the playground to get in line for another handball game.

◇ **ABOUT THE AUTHOR**

Bob Sizoo has taught sixth grade in Eureka, California, since 1986. He is currently on leave from his teaching position to codirect the Redwood Writing Project. He has been a teacher consultant with that National Writing Project site since 1987. He lives in Fieldbrook, California, with his wife, three horses, and two cats.

◇ **NOTES FROM THE AUTHOR**

I tried to show in the story how much I learned from Brandon without telling the reader "Brandon sure taught me a lot." Did you get a sense of this as you heard the story?

Brandon really is one of my heroes. The events that took place in the classroom are pretty much the way I remember them, but the introductory story I made up. The only things I know is that his parents had drug and/or alcohol habits, and they really did take one look at Brandon in the hospital, and left, never to be heard from again. Doctors believe that his incomplete body was caused by his parents' substance abuse. Does my version of the story seem realistic?

◇ **WRITING CHALLENGE: WRITE ABOUT A HERO IN YOUR LIFE**

Think about heroes as defined in the story—"Heroes face all kinds of adversity and show the strength and courage to persevere against enormous odds—to keep trying when the rest of us mere mortals would have given up." Do you know someone who fits that description? Try writing a piece about this person.

Bonus Drawing Challenge:

Try this—tuck a pencil or pen into the crook in your elbow. Now draw a picture or write a message to a friend. This is how Brandon drew the illustration of a dodo.

THE GIFT

◇◇◇◇◇◇◇◇◇◇◇◇◇◇◇◇◇◇◇◇◇

Snakes terrified my mother. Real snakes, plastic snakes, paper snakes. All lengths, thicknesses, varieties. Snakes touched, seen in the backyard, glimpsed in movies or on television, in photographs, paintings and drawings. The thought scared her. Even the word itself.

When I was a boy, I loved westerns. I'd get close to the television and stretch out on my stomach to watch. If my mother was sitting in the room, she wouldn't watch the screen, because sooner or later the cowboy and his horse had to encounter a rattlesnake. Tarzan movies were worse, as the hero usually engaged in a prolonged fight to the death with some bloated python wrapped around his middle.

If she did watch these or some other, more benign, nearly-certain-to-be-snake-free show and a snake appeared on the screen, she let out a single deep-throated scream. Then she flung down anything she might have had in her lap as she leapt to her feet and stormed from the room.

When I was five or six and this happened, I got up and went after her. Usually, I found her in the kitchen, her back to me. She didn't want to talk, didn't want anyone to see her, and if I came up and touched her, she shivered and jerked her body clear. "Don't," she spat. Then remembering who I was she said, more kindly, "Go back and watch TV."

I remember one summer Saturday she was sitting at the table drinking coffee and reading the newspaper. Suddenly, her scream erupted; the paper sailed in one direction, her coffee cup in the other. Hours later she seemed sadly pleased when I told her I'd cut out the offending photograph and thrown it away—I'd have burned it if I'd been allowed to play with matches. And for a time after that—perhaps as long as the rest of the summer—I searched for snakes in the paper every day, before she had a chance to read it. But with snakes, relief was only temporary.

I grew up in the country in western Massachusetts, about five miles outside the town of Great Barrington, population four thousand. Both my parents were born and raised in New York City, so moving to the country when my sister was four and I was six months old must have been a big change for them. Since she didn't work and my father needed our one car for his job, my mother found herself isolated in a house on one acre surrounded entirely by fields and woodland, with shielding mountains obliterating the horizon—from our yard you could look in all directions and not see another house. Pressured by her parents—who moved into the same house along with the rest of us—and struggling to raise two children under their critical eyes, my mother gave up museums and subways and Radio City for a land where, out walking, she was more likely to run across a snake than a neighbor.

To complicate matters, she loved to garden. She was terrific with flowers, and she also had a vegetable garden that got larger every year. She always started out ambitious and energetic, optimistic—did she think, this year the snakes will be gone? Invariably, and usually by the warm weather of late May, she'd be out in her garden and we'd all hear a scream, and we'd look out to see her running, not anywhere in particular, just running from, trying to get as far away as possible from the spot where the snake had shown itself.

After that first snake of the season, my mother would garden sporadically, depending on how courageous she felt. My father tried to help, but he was no

gardener, and no matter how carefully she described what she wanted him to do, he never seemed to do it quite correctly. Besides, the purpose of having the garden was to enjoy working in it, so what enjoyment could she get watching my father from the window?

He served her best as a sentry. I recall coming home, when I was high school and college age, and looking out the window down at the garden, to find my mother on her knees weeding, or squatting to prune the tomatoes, while my father stood at the edge of the garden, holding a long shovel as if it were a lance, poised to charge forward and slay any snake that might rear its menacing head.

Now as an adult looking back, with my father retired and my mother dead ten years, that seems like a noble image. But the fact is, it never worked. If my mother saw a snake, it didn't matter if my father immediately killed it; the fact that it had been there, and she had seen it, was enough to drive her inside for weeks. It wasn't like saying, there was a killer on the loose but we caught him and locked him away.

Why was my mother afraid of snakes? She used to blame it on her father taking her to the zoo when she was eight or nine years old and forcing her to touch a snake. Later they watched a film where a boa constrictor swallowed a live pig, whole. "You could see the outline of the entire pig inside that snake," she said. "It was still moving around, still struggling."

But it turns out that trip to the zoo was something my grandfather did *because* of my mother's fear of snakes. Apparently, she'd been causing trouble in science class because she refused to look at pictures of reptiles (I imagine her science book flung across the room). This was a school that, because she was naturally left-handed, used to tie her left hand to the desk during penmanship, to force her to use her right. So I doubt they had much sympathy for irrational fear.

Maybe, in a strange way, my mother found it useful to fear snakes. In many other aspects of life, she

was a courageous woman, strong and self-sacrificing. Maybe, when she made snakes the single great enemy—the great Satan—all the rest of the world seemed less threatening to her.

Or perhaps it *was* just an irrational fear.

I first learned of that fear the hard way. When I was five, my mother discovered a snake under our front steps. Probably it was a wood snake, which though harmless can grow to an intimidating size. After inspection, my grandfather determined there was a nest of them living beneath the steps, and he and my father set about with axes and shovels to tear apart the steps and destroy that nest of snakes.

Being the only other male in the family, of course, I helped. I wasn't allowed near the axe, and I had only a plastic shovel, but I watched, ready to assist if needed. For a five-year-old boy, anything being violently destroyed is exciting. At some level, I understood there was nothing wrong with the steps themselves, and the snakes could not hurt me; both were being sacrificed for the sake of my mother, who had not left the house since she saw the first one.

My father and grandfather did find a nest, and with axes and shovels flailing, they killed all the snakes. I was thrilled. I wanted my mother to know it was safe now, there was no longer a reason to be afraid. I wanted her to know I'd helped, too. So as they were cleaning up, loading bloody snake bits into the wheelbarrow, I found a head with a bit of neck attached. A streak of blood got on my shovel as I transferred the snake to the plastic. I remember it surprised me; I hadn't thought snakes had blood. I kept back, not hiding but trying to be inconspicuous, until my father and grandfather went off toward the woods, pushing the wheelbarrow filled with broken boards and pieces of snake.

Then I joyfully walked into the house to bring my mother her gift.

◇ ABOUT THE AUTHOR

Mark Farrington is a teacher consultant with the Northern Virginia Writing Project and teaches undergraduate writing at George Mason University and fiction writing in the Part-Time Graduate Writing Program of Johns Hopkins University

◇ NOTES FROM THE AUTHOR

The hardest part for me was not deciding what to put in, but what to leave out. Just writing "my grandfather" triggers a half-dozen images and twice that many stories in my head; even more come up for my mother and my father. I had to make sure every sentence I wrote connected directly back to snakes. If I hadn't, I could have written 20 pages and still not known what I was writing about.

I also had to fight a desire to explain. Other readers helped me most with this aspect, as I have trouble seeing when I am getting in the way of my own story.

Finally, I wanted to make sure this piece had some humor. Much of it is sad, and there was sadness throughout much of my childhood. But there was humor, too, and great amounts of love—though as with my "gift," that love often wasn't expressed in the best way.

◇ NOTES FROM THE EDITOR

The hardest thing to learn as a writer is the amount of care and work you have to put into revision. One of my college professors once told me that a short-story writer she knows revises each of his stories at least 50 times!

Mark and I wrote back and forth many times after he submitted his fine story to me, and he had reworked it many times before I even saw it. On the following page, I've reproduced a two-sentence paragraph from his story and the discussion that went on between us about one little phrase.

◇ WRITING CHALLENGE: SHOW, DON'T TELL

Teachers: You may want to use the next page as an overhead to share with the class. In small groups or with partners, ask your students to discuss and then support or refute my editorial decision to cut the underlined phrase. Note also the casual tone and informal greetings and salutations that would be inappropriate for a business letter, but acceptable for an e-mail. I think this discussion illustrates that when it comes to revision, there is often no one right answer for every reader.

Writers, try this: In a piece you've been working on, find a part where you analyze or tell a lot about a character's actions. See if you can cut out the telling part and show the reader what happens, by using dialogue, descriptive writing, or a combination of both. Read each version to a partner or to your response group, and see which one works best for your audience.

Revision of "The Gift"

"If she did watch these or some other, more benign, nearly-certain-to-be-snake-free show and a snake appeared on the screen, she let out a single deep-throated scream, <u>an 'Aah' which was part terror and part anger at the way her fear had betrayed her.</u> Then she flung down anything she might have had in her lap as she leapt to her feet and stormed from the room."

Mark,
In this paragraph I think you should end the first sentence with a period where the comma
is after the word scream. *I think your explanation after that stalls and detracts from the story…*
let the reader wonder about the possible motives behind your mom's scream.
Bob

Bob,
I have two questions. 1. To me, it's always been important to note the way she felt about having this fear—the sense that her own self is "betraying" her. Does this not come across in the part you want to take out and/or does it not really matter to a reader as much as it mattered to me (it's hard sometimes to distinguish what matters to me the writer vs. what mattered to me the son). 2. Does the action of flinging things with snakes (which is repeated elsewhere) need to be stated to set those other ones up? I guess if your answer to these questions leaves you still wanting to take that part out, then out it should go.
Mark

Mark,
Reply to your reply to my reply to your (etc.)… I think the flinging sentence should stay. I think all the flinging, her deep-throated scream, and all her other seeming overreactions in the story makes us readers wonder about her. I want to speculate about why she would act that way; I don't want to have her possible motivations explained. So, I suggest ending at "scream." and leaving the flinging sentence. And YES, in my own writing it is hard to distinguish between what is emotionally important to me from what is important to the reader. My mom died when I was fairly young (27). When I write about her, I have difficulty getting enough distance from the story to imagine myself as an unknown audience.
Bob

Bob,
Your suggestion(s) sound fine to me. Let's go with them.
Mark

A PLACE TO SLEEP FOR THE NIGHT

The old man's eyes were big and bright. He looked out the window as if seeing the scene he described.

"It was c-o-1-d," he said, dragging out the word cold, "musta been January or February. Some snow was on da ground. I needed a place to stays for the night. In dem days folks wouldn't 'llow a black man to stays on the'ir place at night 'specially if he's a stranger. They was a few that would let you stay in the'ir barn or shed, but not many."

As he continued to gaze out the window, he told us that he had stopped at several houses along the way.

"Some folks wouldn't even give me a drink of water," he remembered, "and not a single one was willin' to let me sleep in the'ir barn. Sos I just kept walkin' and knowin' real hard that the good Lord would take care of me." He told me that shortly after dark he had headed into the woods and soon found a cave where he could stop and rest for the night.

"I was in Tennessee you know, in da hills, lots of caves in 'dem parts, lots of wild animals, too. Mountain lions was pretty common. Sometimes you could hear 'em screamin'. It's a lonesome and fearful sound. Goes right through your soul."

I asked him if he had been afraid. He grinned, "Well, sure I was 'fraid some, but I was cold, and I'd been walkin' for a long time, sos I didn't pay much attention to bein' 'fraid. I just asked the good Lord for a dry, warm place to sleep and sure 'nough, I found a cave."

I wanted to know why he was in Tennessee, and he said he had gone there to find work. He told me how he had taken odd jobs for a year or two in whatever town he happened to come to.

"I'd work in a town for a few months, and when the work seemed to play out, I'd move on. Some towns made it pur-fect-ly clear they didn't want me stayin' on permanent, sos I move on."

He looked at me squarely. "Prejudice is a real thing you know. It was worse then, I think. But, folks was more honest 'bout it."

I nodded and looked away. I had no words of wisdom to offer nor had I ever walked even one step in his shoes. The silence engulfed us like a heavy fog, and for a moment, I feared he wouldn't speak again.

"So tell me about the cave," I said gently, hoping to direct him back to the story.

"Well, I slept there all night, in that cave and stayed warm as could be. I crawled pretty far back in and got away from the wind. I remember feelin' something that felt like a human skull." His gnarly old hands stroked the air, opening and closing at the memory of the fearful thing he had grasped. "I really didn't wants to know for certain what it was, but that's sure what it felt like. Anyways, I's just real thankful that the good Lord had provided me with a place to sleep. He been real good to me you know.

"The next mornin' I crawled out of the cave and started down the main road. I hadn't gone very far when two or three trucks met me head on and nearly run me over. They was goin' real fast. I stopped and listened, and it seemed they halted long 'bout my cave. I turns 'round to go sees what

was all the fuss 'bout."

The old man looked out the window again. He didn't speak for several seconds. Then, taking a deep breath, he continued.

"Just 'fore I got there, I heard guns firin', several at once. I couldn't imagine what was goin' on. There was a big group of peoples there, all standin' 'round the mouth of my cave a lookin' down at somethin'. I tried to ease my way into the crowd, but it wasn't fittin' for a black man to push his way into white folks, sos I stayed back and waited.

"I finally asked an old gentleman what was all the excitement 'bout."

"'Mountain lions,'" he said, "'one of the sheriff's men tracked em here, to this cave. They found a mother and three cubs.'"

His eyes filled with tears as he related the last part of the story to us.

"I remember just turnin' away, not wantin' to see 'dem poor dead lions. A mama and her cubs. It just wasn't right somehow. That mama lion had let me sleep in her cave with her cubs. She gave me a place to sleep when no human would. I just didn't see how it was right that they should kill her like that. I s'pose she had killed some of the'ir livestock or somethin'. But it was just to feed her babies. They'd a done the same for the'ir youngins."

The old man lowered his gray, wrinkled head. I looked out the window and through the blur of my own tears, imagined him looking toward heaven and thanking his good Lord for having watched over him that night. And I could see him, a young man, walking down that Tennessee road, looking for work and a place to sleep for the night.

◇ ABOUT THE AUTHOR

Lacinda Files was born in western Kentucky and has been in Arkansas since 1985. She's married with three great kids and one cat that definitely is not a mountain lion. She has been a teacher for 14 years, the past 11 in gifted education.

She currently teaches gifted and talented students at Smith Elementary in Springdale, Arkansas, and co-teaches a summer writing camp for kids, grades 5 to 8, at the University of Arkansas, called Kidswrite. Lacinda Files has been a teacher consultant for the Northwest Arkansas Writing Project since 1997.

◇ NOTES FROM THE AUTHOR

I always try to keep my ears and eyes open for story ideas. Sometimes an idea is only a "story kernel," another time it may be the whole ear of corn! When this story landed in my lap, it seemed to be cooked, buttered, and ready to eat! It had all the right ingredients: mystery, controversy, emotion, and drama all in an unusual setting. So writing it was easy as pie, right? Not quite. Writing the story so that others could "taste" it as I had turned out to be no easy bake!

I struggled most with the old man's dialect, wanting to make it genuine, but afraid it might be seen as condescending coming from a Southern white! I was concerned that my lack of experience in writing this type of dialect might make the story sound stilted. I did not want to portray my main character as uneducated or foolish, because he was neither.

Another problem I encountered with this story was time and place. Should I tell the story from where and when it happened (in the present tense) or tell it as a first-person recollection? I knew I did not have enough details of the actual setting to tell the story as an authentic, historical event. I deliberately made the setting ambiguous, because I wanted the focus of the story to be the old man's most unusual "bed" and the circumstances that brought him to it.

If I'm to be a writer worth her salt, then I must keep revising a piece as many times as it takes to really get it "done." Finding just the right texture and taste took a long time and was truly a labor. I kept writing, even when the story seemed "half baked," because I know that when the sweetness of words mix together just right, the reader comes back for seconds.

◇ WRITING CHALLENGE: EXPERIMENT WITH VOICE

We all have heard stories from the past from family or friends. These stories often become more dramatic, dangerous, or historically important in their retelling. List as many of these stories as you can in five minutes. Think of events that may have happened last week, last year, or even before you were born. Some stories probably happened to people you will never meet. Don't put down any details, just a title or some key words to help you remember the story later. When you have come up with a list, go back and choose one to write about. Tell the story as if the main character in the story is telling it to you, as Lacinda Files did with the old man's story in "A Place to Sleep for the Night."

BOBBY AND THE STINGRAY

◇◇◇◇◇◇◇◇◇◇◇◇◇◇◇◇◇◇◇

We lived on a tree-lined street of houses with neatly trimmed lawns. Nature, to us, was anything that deviated from that pattern. The field of dirt clods was nature, as was the patch of firs behind the doctor's house. But the most splendid and dangerous wilderness area lay behind the Crawford estate, home to the wealthiest family in town.

The Crawford's backyard was the rock quarry. Outside their door was a full acre of brambles, boulders, trees, and bushes surrounded by ten-foot-high cliffs. As far as we were concerned, it was the greatest backyard ever—an oasis of wildness and excitement. My backyard was fenced on all four sides and contained two pear trees, which shed an endless supply of rotting fruit onto the shabby lawn.

In 1972 Evel Knievel was our god. Sports stars occasionally impressed us, but they just played games. What Evel Knievel did, like ramp-jumping ten tractor-trailer rigs and living to tell about it, was real. Achieving dangerous speeds on our stingray bicycles, we would jump anything that wouldn't run away. Dentists and surgeons did a thriving business in the early seventies due to Evel's influence on us. At some time or another, all of the neighborhood kids had a bone-shattering, tooth-loosening wipe-out, and for most of us that event signaled our early retirement from the daredevil business. All of us, that is, but Bobby Jones. Bobby had scabs on top of scabs. He was positively fearless.

One ninety-degree day in the middle of summer I saw Bobby heading for the Crawford's quarry likely wearing every stitch of clothing he owned. A gaggle of my cronies were following him, talking excitedly about Bobby jumping the cliffs of the quarry on his stingray. I saw a crazy look in Bobby's eyes through his football helmet.

"Them thorns can't punch through all these clothes, and them vines will cushion me just like a haystack." Bobby was sweating hard and small rivulets of perspiration had carved out valleys in the dust on his face. He had the fire; his eyes were wide and his breath was coming fast. He pushed his bicycle up the hill with a determination and sense of purpose I had never seen.

The road behind the quarry was a narrow, twisting one-way down a steep slope. Just above the quarry it leveled off and straightened out. It was a nearly ideal launch pad.

We found a slab of plywood the size of a car door buried in the blackberries below the cliffs. We judged it to be not entirely rotten, and when we lifted it, thousands of crawling things scuttled for cover. Normally our interest in entomology would have prompted us to take a closer look. Today, we were all business.

We dragged the ramp up to the top of the cliffs and propped it up with a pile of forgotten bricks lying nearby. We quickly analyzed the angle of trajectory and ascertained that Bobby had at least a reasonable chance of landing in the bushes. It was perfect.

Bobby gave the ramp a cursory inspection and decided it was safe. Clearly he had lost whatever judgment he had ever possessed. We were in awe. Bobby and the stingray disappeared around one of the many curves above the ramp. Next came a silence thick and heavy as a fog bank followed by the smooth hum of rubber on pavement. Bobby was pushing it hard, winding his pedals as fast as he could. He was infected by a rare madness, and we all felt privileged to witness it.

Launched from the ramp, he sailed up over the

cliff, gaining altitude at an impossible rate. Bobby and his stingray were frozen against the July sun, the chrome of the handlebars glinting and each spoke radiating the sunlight brilliantly. He looked like an angel; I thought he could stay up there forever.

I was wrong. Bobby descended in an arc that brought him into a blackberry patch that was 20 feet deep. His calculated trajectory had been perfect; however, he had grossly underestimated the force with which he would descend, and he had greatly overestimated the buoyancy of Himalayan blackberries. Blackberries are in no way like haystacks. Bobby plunged through the berry vines like a jetliner through the jungle. Upon impact, both tires deflated and his rims flattened to the hubs. Bobby himself narrowly escaped being impaled on the handlebars. He was below us some 40 or 50 feet, buried in the brambles, motionless, a daredevil Icarus fallen back to earth.

We figured he was dead, or at least seriously injured, and were faced with a moral dilemma. The longer we stayed near Bobby's potentially dead body, the more likely we were to get in trouble. On the other hand, if bones were broken or if Bobby had sliced himself open, we would hate to leave before witnessing all of the carnage. Our compulsion toward the morbid won out, and we scrambled excitedly down the loose rocks to where Bobby hung suspended in the bushes.

He wasn't dead. In fact, to our great disappointment, he wasn't hurt at all. He was bound up like a mummy in blackberry vines and his bicycle was a total loss, but he was fine. He hadn't said anything up to this point, but as we approached, we heard him speaking softly to himself, repeating a single word over and over: "Damn, damn, damn."

But Bobby wasn't angry. That word, was for him a mantra, the exclamation of wonder from a boy who had stared into the eye of God. Bobby had transcended to another place and had left the rest of us behind.

It took us a good part of the afternoon to extri-cate Bobby and the remnants of the stingray from the blackberry jungle. After stripping off the several layers of clothing, we were amazed to see Bobby had sustained no scratch. The flood of sweat had washed away the dirt on his face and his skin was so pale it was almost translucent. A certain calm radiated from him. When I envision Lewis and Clark reaching the Pacific, they wear the same placid, invisible smile that Bobby wore that afternoon.

The wheels on the stingray wouldn't turn, a majority of the spokes were broken, the tires were flat, and the frame had snapped at the headset. Nonetheless, Bobby dragged that bike down the hill leaving a serpentine skid mark almost half a mile long. He threw the bike on the junk heap that was his yard and went into his house.

I didn't see Bobby for a few days. His lack of a functioning bicycle had left him behind on most of the neighborhood activities. I had offered him the use of my sister's bike, but it was an empty gesture. I didn't expect him to ride a girl's bike. We rode off to our crawdad excursions and our trips to the swimming pool without him. Somehow he didn't seem to mind. With the famous jump he had outgrown us, and as we rode away, we would see him on his porch deep in thought.

A week after the jump, I went to Bobby's house but the place had an odd, lifeless look about it. All the junk was still in the front yard, but it had been rearranged slightly, and all of the furniture had been moved out. I peered through the window and saw the refrigerator door open, but no light shone from it.

"Last time I rent to hillbillies," said the disgruntled landlord as he loaded Bobby's broken stingray into the pickup with the rest of the junk pile. I wanted to speak up, to claim the stingray as a sacred relic, and build a monument at the top of the quarry to commemorate the greatest single example of the human conquest of nature that I had ever witnessed. The landlord drove off under the groaning pile of junk. He had no idea of the treasure he possessed.

I followed the snaking skid mark back to the quarry. The berry vines were growing back, but two deep ruts still showed where the stingray had landed. The vines would eventually reclaim their dominion, but they hadn't yet. I kicked a rock down from the top of the cliff and heard it clatter below with the hollow ring of a distant memory. "Damn," I thought.

Far to the west the sun descended into the gray waters of the Pacific. The ocean breeze picked up, the air cooling with the day's last light. Below, the Crawford family was swimming. Set against the rosy streaks of the sunset was the aquatic blue glow of the pool house, the Crawfords bathing in their opulence. I didn't envy them anymore. Splashing in the pool they looked small, pathetic, silly. They owned nothing.

◇ **ABOUT THE AUTHOR**

John Scanlon was raised in Corvallis, Oregon, and is currently in his tenth year of teaching at Pendleton High School. He has one kid; a son who just turned two, and another on the way as of this writing. John says that for some reason his writing and fishing time has taken a serious hit in the last two years. He has been a teacher consultant with the Oregon Writing Project at Eastern Oregon University since 1995 and has led several workshops for their Young Writers' conference.

◇ **NOTES FROM THE AUTHOR**

The technique that generated this piece was suggested by one of my colleagues, Rebecca Wilson, at the writing project at Eastern Oregon University. She had us all draw maps of our childhood neighborhoods and mark different significant events/feelings that we associate with those places. I was frankly amazed at the flood of memories that came back to me as I drew the different places on the map. This story was simply going to be a narrative of events as I remembered them, but sort of took on its own life as I wrote it. My brothers and sisters all agree that something like this happened at the rock quarry, but they all think I got the details wrong. What I struggled with the most was trying to get the details and facts straight in my mind. Finally, I gave up. I stopped worrying about telling a true narrative story and let the imaginative parts take over. The result is an imaginative story (fiction) that came out of a real experience. Did a kid in my neighborhood bundle up in the summer heat and jump off the cliffs into the blackberries? You bet. Did it happen exactly like I told it? Well, frankly no.

◇ **WRITING CHALLENGE: USE SETTINGS TO GENERATE STORY IDEAS**

Try using the technique that John used for "Bobby and the Stingray" to generate writing ideas of your own. Draw two maps. The first one should be of your current or former neighborhood. Show buildings, trees, parks, stores, houses, apartment buildings, etc. Draw a second map, this one of your house. Draw this house map as if someone used a chain saw to cut through all the walls of your house at waist level and then lifted the top part off (if you live in a two-story house, you'll have to slice up both floors). The map of your house should show all the walls, inside and out. Architects and builders call this view a "floor plan."

On each of your maps, mark places where stories have occurred. You can put a symbol to mark each story or number the story locations and make a key to remind you what happened at each place. You'll have tons of story ideas by the time you finish these two maps.

SELINA

I left the library early today. Just as I was locking the door, they came up from the vision room: Selina, Raffy, and Marco all together. Most days I stay after school to keep the library open for the kids, and Raffy and Selina come in and wait for me. Selina is homeless, and she and her mother move to a different shelter every week. The bus won't take her there unless someone can meet her, and they won't go to her grandmother's apartment for some other reason that I don't understand. Maybe it has to do with being dropped off and picked up at the same place. Selina stopped going to school for a while because she couldn't get a ride. Then she had really long days alone in a shelter or in her grandmother's empty apartment, if her mother could get her there before going to work herself. Anyway, it isn't far, and I just give her a lift. She is eighteen, and it's not a problem.

If Marco comes to the library, it's usually just to talk. He is used to getting around the city with his cane, and he gets home on his own. Raffy always comes to the library with Selina, and they sit together reading pages of Braille or quizzing one other on vocabulary using a little machine that speaks in a monotone. Sometimes they smooch a little, like the day the teachers were having a book discussion meeting, and they were almost sharing one chair. "You're not invisible you know," I told them when we left, and they giggled.

I took Selina's arm. "Are you ready?" I asked. "You don't mind leaving early today?" She was standing next to Marco.

"Where's Rafael?" she asked. He was standing silently to one side.

I grabbed the end of her cane and pointed it at him, tapping his shin. "He's right here." Raffy didn't smile or say anything.

"He's not talking to me," Selina said softly, as I offered her my right elbow. Usually, Raffy holds onto Selina, but today he took my left elbow instead and kept his distance. Marco followed with his cane. I could hardly fit through the door to the stairs with one of them on each side. "Ladies first," I said as we went out onto the sidewalk. Selina reluctantly led the way. Marco said goodbye and headed off toward the subway. When we were well outside the school I asked Raffy, "Did you have a bad day?"

"Awful," he said, "I don't want to talk about it."

Often when we get outside, we complain together. They might talk about some class they think is not being taught properly or some incident that happened during the day. Like last week when Selina couldn't go into her classroom because of the fight. I had heard there was a stabbing on the fifth floor. The librarian had told me someone said it was "two Spanish kids." Then on the news that night when I heard the name of the "twenty-two-year-old student who stabbed a younger boy with a ballpoint pen," I thought it sounded like one of the Somali students.

The next morning I told a teacher friend who works on the fifth floor, "They shouldn't let them go to high school when they're that old. They should be working or in night school."

"But the other kid had him in a headlock," she said, "That's why he stabbed him with his pen."

"Who was the other kid?" She didn't know. Another teacher told me the stabber was constantly teased and tormented by the other kid. That's when I just suspended judgment of the whole thing.

We walked to my car. Traffic always comes to a

stop when you cross the street with two blind people, and when Raffy is feeling good, he waves his cane and yells out, "President Clinton is crossing the street," and I tell him he should go everywhere with me so I wouldn't have to wait for the lights to change. But he didn't talk today. I led them to the passenger side of the car, and Selina went over to the front door while Raffy moped around near the trunk. I unlocked my door, which opens all the rest, and watched him slowly feel his way along the car and finally get in the back seat.

"I like the seat this way," Selina said putting on her seat belt. It was reclined more than usual, and Selina's head leaned over Raffy's lap in the seat right behind her, her hair nearly touching him. "I wish I had a tape recorder," she said to me. "I like your voice like this."

"It's my cold. I hope it changes back to my old voice tomorrow." As I drove toward the projects where Raffy lives, he reached over and handed Selina a tape. She felt the Braille label and made some comment in Spanish. I thought she was fixing it for him. I put on the radio. Men's voices were singing a beautiful melody with intricate parts and harmonies. "Do you like opera?" I asked.

"Yes," said Raffy, and I turned it up.

"I think it's Italian. Do you understand it?" I picked up a few words.

"A little," Raffy said. I parked around the back of his building where the door was unlocked most of the time. If it wasn't, he could tap his cane on his kitchen window from the stair landing and his little brother would let him in. The radio announcer said it was a madrigal and started to tell a story about Mozart and his wife. I left it on for Selina and got out to walk Raffy to his house. He flipped opened his cane and put his hand on my shoulder. "It's over," he said tragically as we stepped up the curb. "We broke up. No more boyfriend girlfriend."

"Maybe you'll still be friends…"

"No. Not friends. Not anything." I patted his hand on my shoulder and led him to the start of his

steps. He had tears in his voice. Raffy doesn't get around by himself at all. He wasn't born blind; it happened accidentally during brain surgery only five years ago. As I walked back to my car, I decided not to say anything to Selina about Raffy. Selina sometimes confides in me. Usually, after Raffy gets out, while I am driving to her grandmother's apartment, we talk. She tells me about her day, often repeating whole scenes from class. Or she discusses something she is upset about, like the way Raffy acts or some remark a student made in the hall. Sometimes we stop for honey-dip donuts, and I get her sweet light coffee, which she drinks through the stirrer. I am the messy one, dunking my donut and dripping coffee all over the table.

Selina was fiddling with the tape when I got back in the car. She started pulling strands of it out of the clear plastic cassette as we drove off. "He didn't have to give it back," she said, loops and loops of the shiny brown tape covering her lap. A tear came down one cheek.

I fished in my purse. "Here, I have some extra-soft tissues today."

Suddenly, she threw the cassette out the window. I heard it land and the tape streamed after it, all except a piece that got twisted around a knob on the dashboard. The cassette clattered as I went down the road leading out of the projects. Hard to make a good dramatic gesture when you're blind, I thought and started laughing. "We're dragging it. Like we just got married." Selina started to laugh, and I handed her the last curls of tape to throw out. "Maybe we should have left it," I added. "We could just tie up anyone who walks by the car or wrap up another car if they cut us off. We could tie up the street signs when we turn." Now we were both laughing hysterically.

"I broke up with him," Selina said. "Sunday he came over my grandmother's, and I told him. He's not nice to me. But I didn't want the tape back."

◇ **ABOUT THE AUTHOR**

Madeleine Ballard is a teacher in Kentucky and a teacher consultant with the Louisville Writing Project.

◇ **NOTES FROM THE AUTHOR**

I first wrote this story when I got home that day after dropping Selina off. Later, I changed everyone's names, but I still feel a little guilty writing about them. One of the problems I had was how to let the reader know that the students were blind without making that the entire focus of the characters. Also, I didn't want the whole piece to be a description of our actions, but I did want the reader to know what was going on. I guess only you know if I got the balance right.

◇ **WRITING CHALLENGE: GO BEYOND STEREOTYPES**

This story is about blind people, but not about the obvious topic—their blindness, and how they cope with or overcome difficulties. Rather, these things are in the background of the story. Try to write a story about someone you know (or even yourself) that is not about the obvious characteristic of that person. Examples:

• A story about a rich person that is not about money or power.

• A story about a poor person that is not about poverty.

• A story about a great athlete that is not about sports.

• A story about a policeman that is not about police work.

• A story about a soldier that is not about war.

Get the idea?

◇ BY STACEY NAVARRE

HANDS OF LOVE

◇◇◇◇◇◇◇◇◇◇◇◇◇◇◇◇◇◇

The air in the round, cramped visiting room felt close as I sat holding Grandma's worn hand. The hospital-white plaster walls, now slightly yellowed and cracked after years of neglect, stood sparsely decorated with dime-store paintings. Shafts of sunlight slanted through the picture windows neatly framed with honeyed oak molding. The hardwood floors creaked as nurses breezed in and out with medication and food trays, bringing with them a mixed odor of canned vegetables, rubbing alcohol, and disinfectant. People with thin, graying hair, hunched shoulders, and wrinkled skin slouched in their wheelchairs, silently staring at the walls or the TV that droned continuously for no one in particular. Holding her IV monitor clumsily beside her, Elsie, the hospital grump, shuffled past and muttered something to Lester and Buck who were playing another endless game of checkers. I listened to Mabel babble on in the corner about a baby while I watched her fingers move rhythmically, manipulating nothing but air, as she mimicked the act of knitting.

Scooting closer to Grandma's wheelchair, I noticed our own intertwined hands: old and young, calloused and soft, wrinkled and smooth. Grandma's scarred hands mirrored the many years of picking cotton for a few cents per long, arduous day in the hot, dusty fields of central California. My hands reflected my youthful eighteen years and a sheltered life with few hardships. Dad always said I had my Grandma's hands, but at that moment, they seemed so different from hers. I ached to take away those years of pain and adversity, and yet, I felt such admiration toward her strong spirit and stamina. I revered her for enduring such a harsh life: marrying at only seventeen, having six children one right after another, all in a log cabin in the Ozark Mountains, and raising those kids single-handedly while Grandpa was forced to work out of state. The dreams of a better life later took her family to California, only to be crumbled by the hot, dry sun in a cotton field.

Wiping a tear from my cheek, I tried to perk up and said, "I was over at the house this morning. The apple blossoms look so pretty. Mrs. Wells told me to tell you 'hi.'"

Grandma only sat there, silent and staring out the window. In her steel-blue eyes, I saw nothing but blankness, no recognition or sign of understanding. The right side of her mouth, now paralyzed and slightly sagging, made conversation difficult. Occasionally Grandma would talk, but her loss of concentration rendered her unable to speak coherently. So, perhaps out of pride, Grandma rarely uttered a word. Her right hand, now crippled, lay crooked and stiff in her lap. I tried to visualize how her hands must have looked when she was eighteen. I noticed she was still wearing the simple gold wedding ring on her left hand. How pretty her hands must have been when she got married. I envisioned her fingers long and smooth, unlike now with wrinkled folds of skin around the knuckles. I imagined that she didn't bite her nails back then but kept them neatly trimmed. I squeezed her left hand and prayed, "Please God, let her know I'm here."

I remembered how unlike her calloused hands, Grandma's character had always been caring and sweet. She was a constant source of love and security for me, and as far back as my memory could take me, Grandma could never keep her hands away from me.

She loved to grab hold of me, pull me close, and lovingly squeeze me to her chest. I recalled how we would sit for hours with holding hands, gossiping and giggling about her neighbors or discussing our mutually favorite soap opera, "Days of our Lives."

"Did you watch Bo and Hope's wedding on 'Days' yesterday?" I asked.

Trying to communicate, Grandma looked at me and garbled, "Lee, we need to pick them there daisies and can 'em 'fore next spring."

Recalling how Grandma loved to hear about my social life, specifically who the current boyfriend was, I tried again. "Grandma, I met a guy at school; his name is Dave. We met at this dance and he's from—"

"Leslie, now I want y'all to go on out there and get them there shovels and cut down that there fence," Grandma interrupted, pulling her left hand from mine and agitatedly twisting at her gown.

I smoothed her thin gray hair, severely pulled back on the sides with bobby pins and then rested my head on her shoulder. Holding and stroking her hand again, my mind began wandering back to another time I sat holding Grandma's hand. As an enthusiastic kindergartner who had just mastered the act of writing the alphabet, I had been surprised and confused to learn that not only had Grandma never gone to school, but that she could not write her name, let alone the alphabet. I embraced the opportunity to help my grandma, and with excitement and determination, I set out to teach her to write. I remembered her warm, sweaty hand in mine as we meticulously traced the letters together. When we had finished, we were so proud of each other; we had just smiled and sighed happily at our hard work.

But I remembered Grandma had taught me many things, too. I recalled how much I had loved her buttermilk biscuits, and feeling confident after two years of cooking projects in 4–H, I had been pretty sure that I could learn how to make them for myself. However, never being taught standardized measurement, Grandma used her fingers and hands instead of measuring cups and spoons to make the dough (a much different form of cooking than my 4–H leader had taught me). After many errors and more trials, I finally had been able to make a batch that was edible, but they never came close to the buttery rich taste of Grandma's.

The sun started to fall behind the large oak trees, bringing me out of my reminiscence as shadows appeared on the walls and the air began to chill. I reached around Grandma's back and pulled her quilt out from behind her. Draping it over her bare legs, I noticed its starred shapes of various patterned fabrics and the delicately hand-sewn stitches. Besides her children, making quilts had always been Grandma's source of pride. She would take her old dresses and remnant fabrics and make the most beautiful blankets with such intricate patterns and detail. I recalled as a child, watching with fascination as her fingers carefully guided the needle in and out of the fabric, painstakingly connecting the shapes of cloth with tiny, invisible stitches. Every one of her children and each grandchild had at least one of her quilts, and we regarded them as works of love. I thought of the quilt she had made for me now resting on my own bed at home and how during the past year I had agonized over Grandma's inevitable departure. I found solace in that quilt; laying beneath it, I would feel the same security and love I had felt as a child sleeping in her arms.

Thinking of my quilt, I proudly announced, "Grandma, you remember a couple years ago when you got me started on that quilt? Well, I finally finished it last week. It's pretty good, but not nearly as beautiful as the ones you make."

For the first time that day, Grandma turned and looked at me. With brilliance and clarity, she saw me, and as tears gathered in the corners of her eyes, she smiled.

Frozen, I sat staring at Grandma's beautiful face. Choking on the tightening knot in my throat,

I managed to promise, "Next time I visit, I'll bring my quilt for you."

Using her good hand, she squeezed my arm and said, "I'd love that."

With trembling lips, I kissed Grandma's cheek.

Pulling her quilt around us both, I nestled next to her warm body. I sat like that for a long time, wrapped in Grandma's arms, feeling her tired, loving hands on my back, holding me, and loving me.

◇ ABOUT THE AUTHOR

Stacey Navarre lives in Arcata, California, where she teaches seventh and eighth grade literature at Pacific Union Elementary School. She has been a teacher-consultant with The Redwood Writing Project since 1995. She happily lives with her husband, Dave, and two children, Brittany and Jake. While Stacey doesn't have time to create her own quilts, she does collect them, thanks to her grandma.

◇ NOTES FROM THE AUTHOR

This story has gone through quite a metamorphosis; even now as I read it again, I can think of numerous things I would like to add, delete, or change. The original draft was fairly dry and objective, as if an outsider was reporting the event. As I went from that draft to another, and then another, the piece evolved. It got more personal as recollections of my grandma crystallized in my memory and took shape on paper—soon the only thing left of the "incident" was the introduction to a first-hand biographical sketch about Grandma. The rest of the piece is a collection of my favorite memories of my grandma. Like her quilts, I now have this biographical sketch to save and pass on to my own children—her great-grandchildren.

Vocabulary Lesson: Oftentimes, when we read or hear unfamiliar words in a story, we can figure out the meaning by looking at the context in which they're used. On the next page are six sentences from "Hands of Love" that contain words your students may not know. Make the page into an overhead, duplicate a few copies for small group work, or put the sentences on the board. Ask your students to determine the definition of the underlined words, giving evidence based on the context in which they are used.

◇ WRITING CHALLENGE: REVISE FOR WORD CHOICE

One way to spice up your writing and avoid clichés is to use a thesaurus while you revise. A thesaurus can help you say exactly what you want to say, but if you're not careful and use a word you're unfamiliar with, you can change the meaning of your sentence to one that says something different than you intend.

Here's an example of how I used a thesaurus while editing. In "Hands of Love," Stacey Navarre tells of her grandmother's early life as she writes, "The dreams of a better life later took her family to California, only to be crumbled by the hot, dry sun in a cotton field." Originally, the sentence had the word *shattered* instead of *crumbled,* and I didn't like that word. I couldn't see the sun shattering something. I thought that when you put something in the sun too long, it dries up and dies. So I looked up *dry* and got to *withered,* which I liked. But Grandma's dream didn't just wither, it died, too. So I looked up *wither,* that took me to *disintegrate,* which wasn't quite right, either, but closer to what I was looking for. I looked up *disintegrate* and that gave me *crumble,* which seemed just right to me. I made the suggestion to the author, and she liked it, too. What do you think about that choice? Would you have used a different word?

Revise a piece of your writing using a thesaurus. Find some parts in your piece where you have used a cliché, or where you've used a word or phrase that doesn't say exactly what you mean. Use the thesaurus to make the meaning more precise. Be careful to not use words that you don't know, or you may end up saying something you don't mean at all.

Vocabulary in Context

Sample sentences from "Hands of Love" by Stacey Navarre

1. Grandma's scarred hands mirrored the many years of picking cotton for a few cents per long, <u>arduous</u> day in the hot, dusty fields of central California.

2. I ached to take away those years of pain and <u>adversity</u>, and yet, I felt such admiration toward her strong spirit and stamina.

3. I revered her for <u>enduring</u> such a harsh life: marrying at only seventeen, having six children one right after another, all in a log cabin in the Ozark Mountains, and raising those kids single-handedly while Grandpa was forced to work out of state.

4. I <u>envisioned</u> her fingers long and smooth, unlike now with wrinkled folds of skin around the knuckles.

5. She would take her old dresses and <u>remnant</u> fabrics and make the most beautiful blankets with such intricate patterns and detail.

6. I found <u>solace</u> in that quilt; laying beneath it, I would feel the same security and love I had felt as a child sleeping in her arms.

RESOURCES TO ENRICH YOUR TEACHING

Join the summer institute at the National Writing Project near you. Ask your colleagues if they've attended or contact the NWP.
On the web: www.writingproject.org
E-mail: nwp@writingproject.org
Phone: (510) 642-0963

GREAT BOOKS ABOUT TEACHING WRITING

Reading any book on this list will improve your teaching. Guaranteed.

Atwell, Nancie. *In the Middle.* (second edition) Heinemann, 1998. The bible for teaching reading and writing in middle school. Get it.

Calkins, Lucy. *The Art of Teaching Writing.* Heinemann, 1994. Aimed at kindergarten through sixth-grade teachers. Even with a heavy primary focus, Lucy Calkins, a kidwatcher in the tradition of Donald Graves, reminds us that good, child-centered teaching strategies stretch across the grade levels.

Fletcher, Ralph and Portalupi, Joann. *Craft Lessons: Teaching Writing K–8.* Stenhouse, 1998. A great collection of mini-lessons specifically addressing the writer's craft. Even though this book is divided into grade levels and only one third of the lessons are in the fifth- through eighth-grade section, with very little modification all of the lessons can be used with middle schoolers. (Remember, learning to write is a recursive journey through the writing process.)

Fletcher, Ralph. *What a Writer Needs.* Heinemann, 1993. A fine book to read to improve your own writing as well as that of your students. Ralph Fletcher is an accomplished writer and speaks like a writer, and has spent a lot of time in classrooms and speaks like a teacher. He brings to life his lessons on elements of writing in a way that

seems like he's sitting on the other side of your kitchen table sharing a pot of tea with you.

Graves, Donald. In nearly all the other books on this list, Donald Graves' work is acknowledged. His book *Writing: Teachers and Children at Work* (Heinemann, 1983) has been reprinted at least 17 times and is more responsible for the teaching of writing as a process in our schools than any other single publication. *A Fresh Look at Writing* (Heinemann, 1994) translates the ideas behind teaching writing as a process into "actions" a teacher can take in his or her classroom. I could list 10 more books.

Harwayne, Shelly. *Lifetime Guarantees.* Heinemann, 2000. Even though this book is based on work in a K–5 school, you'll find no better picture of what a literate classroom can look like at any grade level. Her book, *Going Public* (Heinemann, 1999) shows just what can happen when an entire school (in this case, Manhattan New School) dedicates itself to improving student literacy. Without giving away the plot, I can tell you that the purchase of expensive test-prep materials was not involved.

Murray, Donald. When Don Graves acknowledges someone in a book, it's Donald Murray. His writing helps me think like a writer. I recommend *Shoptalk* (Heinemann, 1991) and *Write to Learn* (Harcourt Brace, 1996). Warning: If you start reading his work, you'll get hooked. If you get the *Boston Globe,* read his weekly column, *Over Sixty.*

Routman, Regie. *Conversations.* Heinemann, 2000. This book picks up where the great *Invitations* (Heinemann, 1994) left off. Regie Routman is a kids' advocate first, and argues persuasively that if we want out students to become lifelong learners than we'd better view teaching as learning. Her prose makes me excited about teaching and anxious to get back to my classroom. The "Blue Pages" section has so many tools and resources that it alone would be worth the price of the book.

Schaefer, Lola M. *Teaching Narrative Writing.* Scholastic, 2001. A fine collection of lessons, organizers, and rubrics, many of which are useful for teaching personal narrative and all of which can be used when teaching other forms of narrative.

OTHER BOOKS CONTAINING AUTOBIOGRAPHICAL INCIDENTS

Graves, Donald. *How to Catch a Shark.* Heinemann, 1998.

Spinelli, Jerry. *Knots in My Yo-Yo String.* Knopf, 1998.

OTHER USEFUL BOOKS

Hall, Susan. *Using Picture Storybooks to Teach Literary Devices.* Oryx Press, 1990 (vol. 1) and 1994 (vol. 2). Good reference.

Lamott, Anne. *Bird by Bird.* Anchor, 1995. Become a better writer and get a few yucks along the way. Read it.

Stiggins, Richard J. *Student-Involved Classroom Assessment.* Prentice Hall, 2001. Nuts and bolts of getting your students involved in assessing themselves, not just in writing, but in all subject areas.

Trelease, Jim. *The New Read-Aloud Handbook.* Penguin, 1995. The king of reading aloud. If you need to find justification for reading aloud to your students, here it is.

Appendices

SIGN-UP FOR AUTHOR'S CHAIR

Name	Title of Piece	Genre	Time Required to Read Aloud

Teaching Powerful Writing / Scholastic Professional Books

PEER RESPONSE FORM

Name _____ Author's Name _____

Title of Piece _____

+	- / ?

SIGN-UP FOR PEER RESPONSE

Name	Title of Piece/Genre	Date	I've read this piece aloud (yes/no)

WRITING ASSESSMENT SCALE

6 — Exceptional Writer

- You enjoy writing and often write on your own.
- Your writing often shows many of the same literary elements professional writers use, such as symbolism, metaphor, simile, personification, fully developed characters, clearly described settings, universal themes, foreshadowing, dialogue, irony, alliteration, and humor.
- Your writing is lively, original, and descriptive.
- You write to many audiences and for many purposes.
- Your writing reads smoothly and is organized; it seems to have been "planned out."
- You carefully choose and arrange your words and phrases.
- Your spelling, grammar, and punctuation are nearly perfect.
- You want to revise and edit your writing often to make it the best you can.
- You revise and edit in many ways.
- You "show" with your writing instead of "telling."

5 — Strong Writer

- You sometimes use the techniques of an exceptional writer (above).
- You are a confident writer.
- Your writing is well organized.
- Your sentences are clear, whole, and vary in length.
- You usually "show" rather than "tell" with your writing.
- You have few errors in spelling, grammar, and punctuation.
- You are willing to revise and edit.

4 — Capable Writer

- You are comfortable with writing.
- You are beginning to use techniques of an exceptional writer (above).
- Your writing shows that you had a plan.
- You vary the length and arrangement of your sentences.
- You are beginning to use exact vocabulary, but there is more telling than showing in your writing.
- You may make some errors in spelling, grammar, and punctuation.
- Your writing improves when you revise.

3 — Developing Writer

- You are beginning to become confident in your writing.
- You are becoming more able to put your thoughts down on paper.
- Your writing sometimes seems like it is not organized.
- Your sentences often sound very much alike.
- You use few words to describe.
- You make errors in spelling, grammar, and punctuation, but your writing is readable.

2 — Basic Writer

- You do put words into sentences.
- You may not be excited about writing, but you can spell basic words.
- Your writing often seems like you didn't plan it out.
- Sometimes it isn't clear what you're trying to say.
- Problems with spelling and punctuation make your writing hard for others to read.

1 — Beginning Writer

STUDENT SELF-ASSESSMENT: WRITING

Name _____   Date _____

I am a level _____ writer. I know this because I:

In order to become a level _____ writer, I need to improve the following skills:

WRITING ASSESSMENT RUBRIC

Attribute	Very Successful	Moderate Success	Some Success	No Success	Points
1					
2					
3					
4					
5					
6					
7					
8					
9					
10					

Genre _____

WRITING ASSESSMENT RUBRIC

Attribute	Very Successful	Moderate Success	Some Success	No Success	Points
1 Strong beginning	3	2	1	0	
2 Good flow to story	5	4	3	0	
3 Lots of showing writing: Little telling	5	4	3	0	
4 Good use of dialogue	5	4	3	0	
5 Shows the importance of event to author	4	3	2	0	
6 Setting: "Puts the reader in the story"	5	4	3	0	
7 Creates suspense	4	3	2	0	
8 Good flow — the reader doesn't get lost	5	4	3	0	
9 Includes sensory details	3	2	1	0	
10 We know what the author feels and why	3	2	1	0	

Genre _____

PROVE IT!

On this page, give at least four pieces of evidence from your writing
that show how you arrived at your score on the rubric. Be specific!

For Attribute _____ , I would point to page _____ paragraph _____ . You can see I

For Attribute _____ , I would point to page _____ paragraph _____ . You can see I

For Attribute _____ , I would point to page _____ paragraph _____ . You can see I

For Attribute _____ , I would point to page _____ paragraph _____ . You can see I

For Attribute _____ , I would point to page _____ paragraph _____ . You can see I

For Attribute _____ , I would point to page _____ paragraph _____ . You can see I

On the back, explain what you learned from working on this piece, and what
you plan to work on to make your next piece of writing even better.